T0215192

COGNITIVE DESIGN FOR ARTIFICIAL MINDS

Cognitive Design for Artificial Minds explains the crucial role that human cognition research plays in the design and realization of artificial intelligence systems, illustrating the steps necessary for the design of artificial models of cognition. It bridges the gap between the theoretical, experimental, and technological issues addressed in the context of AI of cognitive inspiration and computational cognitive science.

Beginning with an overview of the historical, methodological, and technical issues in the field of cognitively inspired artificial intelligence, Lieto illustrates how the cognitive design approach has an important role to play in the development of intelligent AI technologies and plausible computational models of cognition. Introducing a unique perspective that draws upon Cybernetics and early AI principles, Lieto emphasizes the need for an equivalence between cognitive processes and implemented AI procedures, in order to realize biologically and cognitively inspired artificial minds. He also introduces the Minimal Cognitive Grid, a pragmatic method to rank the different degrees of biological and cognitive accuracy of artificial systems in order to project and predict their explanatory power with respect to the natural systems taken as a source of inspiration.

Providing a comprehensive overview of cognitive design principles in constructing artificial minds, this text will be essential reading for students and researchers of artificial intelligence and cognitive science.

Antonio Lieto is a researcher in Artificial Intelligence at the Department of Computer Science of the University of Turin, Italy, and a research associate at the ICAR-CNR in Palermo, Italy. He is the current Vice-President of the Italian Association of Cognitive Science (2017–2022) and an ACM Distinguished Speaker on the topics of cognitively inspired AI and artificial models of cognition.

COGNITIVE DESIGN FOR ARTIFICIAL MINDS

Antonio Lieto

 Routledge
Taylor & Francis Group

LONDON AND NEW YORK

First published 2021
by Routledge
2 Park Square, Milton Park, Abingdon, Oxon OX14 4RN

and by Routledge
52 Vanderbilt Avenue, New York, NY 10017

Routledge is an imprint of the Taylor & Francis Group, an informa business

British Library Cataloguing-in-Publication Data
A catalogue record for this book is available from the British Library

Library of Congress Cataloging-in-Publication Data
Names: Lieto, Antonio, 1983– author.
Title: Cognitive design for artificial minds / Antonio Lieto.
Description: Abingdon, Oxon ; New York, NY : Routledge, 2021. |
Includes bibliographical references and index.
Identifiers: LCCN 2020048017 (print) | LCCN 2020048018 (ebook)
Subjects: LCSH: Cognition. | Artificial intelligence.
Classification: LCC BF311 .L536 2021 (print) | LCC BF311 (ebook) |
DDC 153.3—dc23
LC record available at https://lccn.loc.gov/2020048017
LC ebook record available at https://lccn.loc.gov/2020048018

ISBN: 978-1-138-20792-9 (hbk)
ISBN: 978-1-138-20795-0 (pbk)
ISBN: 978-1-315-46053-6 (ebk)

Typeset in Bembo
by codeMantra

CONTENTS

List of illustrations   *vii*
Introduction   *ix*
Acknowledgements   *xiii*

1 Cognitive science and artificial intelligence: death and rebirth of a collaboration   1
When Cognitive Science was AI 1
From the general problem-solver to the society of mind: cognitivist insights from the early AI era 2
Heuristics and AI eras 9
Modelling paradigms and AI eras: cognitivist and emergentist perspectives 10
Death and rebirth of a collaboration 18

2 Cognitive and machine-oriented approaches to intelligence in artificial systems   20
Nature- vs. machine-inspired approaches to artificial systems 20
Functionalist vs. structuralist design approaches 21
Levels of analysis of computational systems 24
The space of cognitive systems 30
Functional and structural neural systems 32
Functional and structural symbolic systems 34

3 Principles of the cognitive design approach   37
Classical, bounded, and bounded-rational models of cognition 37
Resource-rationality models 40
Kinds of explanations 43
Levels of plausibility and the minimal cognitive grid (MCG) 48

4 **Examples of cognitively inspired systems and application of the Minimal Cognitive Grid** 52

Modern AI systems: cognitive computing? 52
Cognitive architectures 57
SOAR 61
ACT-R 63
Two problems for the knowledge level in cognitive architectures 65
Knowledge size and knowledge heterogeneity in SOAR and ACT-R 69
DUAL PECCS 72

5 **Evaluating the performances of artificial systems** 77

"Thinking" machines and Turing Test(s) 77
The Chinese Room 83
The Newell test for a theory of cognition 85
The Winograd Schema Challenge 87
DARPA challenges, RoboCup, and RoboCup@Home 89
Comparison 90

6 **The next steps** 93

The road travelled 93
The way forward 95
Towards a standard model of mind/common model of cognition 103
Community 104

References 107
Index 117

ILLUSTRATIONS

Figures

1.1 Overview of the internal dynamics of physical symbol systems
(adapted from Vernon, 2014)   12
1.2 Brooks' Subsumption Architecture (adapted from Brooks, 1999)   17
2.1 Enriched 2D space of cognitive systems   30
4.1 The SOAR cognitive architecture, from Laird (2012), with
permission from MIT Press   62
4.2 The ACT-R cognitive architecture (permission from Elsevier)   64
4.3 An example of the hybrid conceptual architecture in
DUAL PECCS   73
5.1 A pictorial representation of the "Imitation game"   79

Tables

4.1 Newell's timescale of human actions   63
4.2 Prototype models vs exemplar models   68
5.1 Comparative table of the different evaluation approaches   91

INTRODUCTION

This book is about (re)building a bridge between two different "sciences of the artificial" – Artificial Intelligence and Cognitive Science – that, nowadays, apart from some notable exceptions, do not talk as much with each other as they should. Here, I review some of the main themes that have characterized the historical paths of these two disciplines and argue that the technological maturity reached in several domains now calls for a renewed joint enterprise aimed at addressing more substantial challenges that these two disciplines have to face from a scientific viewpoint.

The book explicitly targets a multidisciplinary audience. As such, it is mainly an act of courage (or probably of irresponsibility), since experts in the specific subfields of AI and Cognitive Science will have for sure much more to say and would surely be able to communicate their own ideas in a better way than I can. However, as mentioned, this book privileges the breath of the connections between the disciplines rather than the depths of the exploration within each single discipline. As such, it is not a manual or a handbook since it presupposes the knowledge of same basic elements of each discipline that will be touched upon by our arguments. Of course, scholars and students of the diverse fields have knowledge of different pieces of the entire puzzle and need to be briefly introduced to the aspects they do not know. This service is provided in the book, though we direct the reader towards specialized literature for details.

One of the main goals of this manuscript is to show the reader that the so-called "cognitive design approach" has still an important role to play in the development of intelligent AI technologies as well as in the context of development of plausible computational models of cognition. In other words, the study of the "Cognitive Design" principles for building "Artificial Minds" will be hopefully a useful instrument for current and future generations of AI and cognitive science scholars and students. In this respect, a caveat is necessary: in the philosophical literature on AI there are many different, and well-known, positions about whether or not it is justifiable to use the terms "mind", "intelligence", or "thinking" to describe the constitutive or the behavioural elements of a computational system. In this book we will not foray into the details of such a monumental and decades-long debate, which also involves the attribution of such faculties to other "species" (from non-human mammals to bacteria). Given the actual purpose of the book, we will also avoid roughly summarizing it because such an attempt would be necessarily incomplete. Sometimes, however, we will refer to some instances of such a debate. For the moment, we will just mention here, as a reference for the position of why the term "mind" can be justifiably associated with the term "artificial", the book *Artificial Minds* by Stan Franklin (Franklin, 1995). The position defended by Franklin – which sees the possession of a "mind" as a matter of degrees and not as a mere Boolean notion and that, as such, foresees the possibility of implementing (to some degree) a "mind" in an artificial system – can be considered our starting working hypothesis.

In Chapter 1, I review the main historical points of contact between AI and cognitive research by briefly introducing early cognitively inspired systems and paradigms and the main factors that led to a "paradigm shift" in the research agendas of these two disciplines starting from the mid-1980s. The reasons for the current renewed interest of a cognitively inspired approach in AI research are discussed. Chapter 2 introduces the main differences between AI systems of "cognitive" inspiration and AI systems that adopt machine-oriented methods to solve specific problems, and proposes a first design distinction between "functional" and "structural" models. It additionally introduces the reader to the debate over the levels of analysis of computational systems (whether they are cognitively inspired or not). The third chapter analyzes the main theories of rational behaviour developed so far and their influence in the realization of rational artificial models. As for the different types of "functional" and "structural" models introduced in Chapter 2, different types of explanatory accounts are provided. Finally, the chapter presents the "Minimal Cognitive Grid" (MCG), a pragmatic methodological tool proposed to rank the different degrees of accuracy of artificial systems built according to the "structural" design perspective in order project and predict their explanatory power with respect to the natural systems that are taken as source of inspiration. The MCG is practically tested in Chapter 4, through the analysis of different types of artificial systems (cognitively inspired and not), ranging from the IBM Watson and Alpha Go, to cognitive architectures like SOAR and ACT-R to artificial models of cognition like DUAL PECCS (a commonsense conceptual categorization system that I have developed over the last few years at the University of Turin, in collaboration with my colleagues Daniele Radicioni and Valentina Rho). The analysis concerning DUAL PECCS and its comparison with the ACT-R and SOAR cognitive architectures is mainly based on a published paper: "The Knowledge Level in Cognitive Architectures: Current Limitations and Possible Developments" (that I co-authored with Christian Lebiere and Alessandro Oltramari), which appeared in 2018 in the journal *Cognitive Systems Research*. Chapter 5 proceeds by providing a comparison of the different types of evaluation approaches proposed in AI and cognitive science and finalized at individuating the degree of "intelligence" or "cognitive compliance" of artificial systems. After the introduction of the Turing Test and of some of its variations, the chapter analyzes the Winograd Schema Challenge and Newell Test for a theory of cognition along with some challenges organized by the international scientific community like the RoboCup World Soccer and the RoboCup@Home. Such approaches, partially having different purposes, will be compared with the proposed MCG. Finally, Chapter 6 concludes the journey by suggesting current and future areas of possible collaboration between AI and Cognitive Science.

ACKNOWLEDGEMENTS

I am indebted to a number of friends and colleagues with whom I have discussed during the past few years the issues presented here. First, I would like to thank my friend and mentor Marcello Frixione for having read and discussed with me different chapters of the manuscript and for having encouraged me to pursue this project. Thanks also to Gian Luca Pozzato for the feedback provided on earlier versions of the book and for his support and friendship. I would like to express my gratitude also to Roberto Cordeschi, who profoundly influenced my training and my research. His book *The Discovery of the Artificial* has been a reference point all these years, as well as during the writing of this. I am also indebted to my colleagues at Dipartimento di Informatica of the University of Turin (Università di Torino) and at the ICAR-CNR of Palermo for the formal and informal discussions (and for the pertinent and impertinent comments) received over the years. In particular, I thank Agnese Augello, Angelo Cangelosi, Antonio Chella, Salvatore Gaglio, Ignazio Infantino, Leonardo Lesmo, Umberto Maniscalco, Giovanni Pilato, Daniele Radicioni, Valentina Rho, and Filippo Vella for the useful discussions concerning our common lines of research. I am also indebted to Cristina Bosco, Rossana Damiano, Roberto Esposito, Vincenzo Lombardo, Alessandro Mazzei, and Viviana Patti for the informal but useful discussions about some themes presented in this book.

Over the last few years I have had also the luck of organizing and being invited to discuss some of these ideas in international forums and events. As for the organizational part, I thank the participants of the panel "Can AI and Cognitive Science still live together happily ever after?" held in 2017 during the XV international conference of AI*IA (the Italian Association for Artificial Intelligence) in Bari (http://aiia2017.di.uniba.it/index.php/joint-panel-aiia-and-aisc/). In particular, I thank Amedeo Cesta, Antonio Chella, Fabio Paglieri, Oliviero Stock, and Giuseppe Trautteur for their active participation. I also thank the participants of the symposium "Advances in Artificial Intelligence and Cognition", organized at the EuroCogsci 2015, as well as the panelists of the round table on "Cognitive approaches to AI" organized during the mid-term conference of AISC (the Italian Association of Cognitive Science) in Genova in 2017. So thank you to Giuseppe Boccignone, Cristiano Castelfranchi, Giulio Sandini, and Amanda Sharkey. Thank you also to all the participants of the workshop series on Artificial Intelligence and Cognition (AIC) – www.aicworkshopseries.org – which has now become an annual appointment for discussing these issues.

My gratitude goes also to Mehul Bhatt, Irene-Anna Diakidoy, Christian Freksa, Oleksandra Gumenna, Ismo Koponen, Antonis Kakas, Kai-Uwe Kühnberger, Amy Loufti, Loizos Michael, Alexei Samsonovich, Alessandro Saffiotti, and Guglielmo Tamburrini for their kind invitations to the Universities of Bremen, Cyprus, Helsinki, Kiev (NAUKMA), Moscow (MEPHI), Napoli, Örebro, and Osnabrück. The comments received during these occasions have been really important for shaping this book.

I have also discussed most of the issues presented here during my visiting period at Carnegie Mellon University and at Lund University. In particular, I am indebted to the feedback received from David Danks, Christian Lebiere, and Alessando Oltramari while at CMU, and from Christian Balkenius and Peter Gärdenfors during my staying at Lund.

Some relevant feedback for the book was also collected during the course "Design and Evaluation of Cognitive Artificial Systems", which I have been teaching over the last few years within the Ph.D. program in Computer Science at the University of Turin. In particular, I would like to thank Narges Azizifard, Elena Battaglia, Andrea Bragagnolo, Davide Colla, Francesco Di Mauro, Manuel Gentile, Valeria Proietti Dante, Gabriele Sartor, and Mirko Zaffaroni.

Writing a book requires so much effort that it is not sufficient to only thank colleagues and friends, since an enormous role of support is played by the family. Therefore, I want to thank my dad Andrea, my mum Anna, my sister Teresa, and my brother Nicola for their support, love, and comprehension. Last, but not least, I owe my deepest thanks to my wife Paola and my daughter Francesca. This book is dedicated to them.

A Paola e Francesca

1

COGNITIVE SCIENCE AND ARTIFICIAL INTELLIGENCE

Death and rebirth of a collaboration

Abstract

The first chapter proposes a brief historical overview of some of the main insights developed over 65 years of research in Artificial Intelligence (AI), by introducing the early vision of the discipline (based on a mutual collaboration with Cognitive Psychology) and its "paradigm shift", which started from the mid-1980s of the last century. Starting from that period on, AI and the interdisciplinary enterprise known as Cognitive Science started to produce several sub-fields, each with its own goals, methods, and criteria for evaluation. The reasons for the current renewed interest of a cognitively inspired approach in AI research are discussed.

When Cognitive Science was AI

Cognitive Science and Artificial Intelligence (AI) are, nowadays, scientific research fields each endowed with a specific autonomy and research agenda. According to the Oxford Dictionary, the term "Artificial Intelligence" is defined as "the theory and development of computer systems able to perform tasks normally requiring human intelligence, such as visual perception, speech recognition, decision-making, and translation between languages", while "Cognitive Science" is defined as "the study of thought, learning, and mental organization, which draws on aspects of psychology, linguistics, philosophy, and computer modelling".

Despite the current different focuses and objectives of each, these two disciplines have many common interests and share the idea of studying the "mind", its emergent properties, and its functioning in natural and artificial systems, respectively.

The history of these two research fields is, in fact, strongly interconnected. Research in AI – the birth of which dates back to the now-legendary "Dartmouth Workshop" (McCarthy et al., 1955) held in the summer of 1956[1] – has, indeed, been historically inspired by the experimental research in psychology.[2] Notable examples of such intellectual connections are represented by the early AI systems/frameworks developed until the 1980s. Most of them, indeed, were explicitly designed with a "cognitively oriented" inspiration. In the following sections, we briefly present few famous examples of such systems and formalisms (though the list is far from being exhaustive) with the aim of introducing some of the main modelling paradigms and assumptions that have characterized, and still characterize, the research in AI and cognitive modelling. Each of the systems/formalisms reviewed below can be considered important either because they have achieved some important milestones in terms of performances or because has introduced some relevant ideas that have fostered meaningful developments in the study and the realization of "artificial minds".

From the general problem-solver to the society of mind: cognitivist insights from the early AI era

One of the first developed AI systems, at the end of the 1950s, is the pioneering work of Herbert Simon, John Clifford Shaw, and Allen Newell on the *General Problem Solver* (GPS). GPS was a system able to demonstrate simple logic theorems and its decision strategies were explicitly inspired by human verbal protocols[3] (Newell, Shaw & Simon, 1959). The underlying idea of this approach was that the computer system had to approximate the decision operations described by humans in their verbal descriptions as closely as possible. In this way, when the program ran on the computer, it would be possible to identify its problems, compare them with the description of the human verbalization, and modify them to improve its performance. In particular, the GPS system was able to implement a key mechanism in human problem solving: the well-known "means-ends analysis" (or M-E heuristics). The M-E heuristics implemented in GPS works as follows: the problem solver makes a comparison between the current

---

1 The organisers of this even were some "giants" of the history of the Computer Science field from the last century: John McCarthy, Marvin Minsky, Nathaniel Rochester, and Claude Shannon. The workshop, during which McCarthy proposed the use of the term "artificial intelligence" to identify the new emerging discipline, ran for several weeks and saw the participation of many researchers. The notes taken by Ray Solomonoff (one of the participants at the workshop) are available online at http://raysolomonoff.com/dartmouth/.
2 It must be noted that, at that time, there wasn't a "Cognitive Science" field. However, all the disciplines (philosophy, psychology, computer science, anthropology, linguistics, and neurophysiology) and the cultural elements that would have later be called upon to form the interdisciplinary field of "Cognitive Science" were already present.
3 This technique is also known as the "thinking aloud protocol" in the psychological literature (Ericsson & Simon, 1980) and consists of recording the verbal explanations provided by people while executing a given laboratory task.

situation and a goal situation; then, it computes and evaluate the "distance" between these two states and tries to find, in memory, suitable operators able to reduce such difference. Once a suitable operator is found, it is then applied to change the current situation. The process is repeated until the goal is gradually attained via a process of progressive distance reduction. There are, however, generally no guarantees that the process will succeed. This kind of heuristic was also used to solve, in the decades to come, problems in a number of domains. In order to be executed, in fact, it "only" required an explicit domain representation of the problem to solve (a problem space), operators to move through the space, and information about which operators were relevant for reducing which differences.[4] GPS can be arguably considered the first cognitively inspired AI system ever developed.

A decade after the development of GPS, a Ph.D. student of Herbert Simon[5] at Carnegie Mellon University (then still named Carnegie Institute of Technology) – Ross Quillian – developed another influential idea in the context of AI of cognitive inspiration; he invented the *Semantic Networks*: a psychologically plausible model of human semantic memory implemented in a computer system. The idea (Quillian, 1968) was that human memory is associative in nature and that concepts are represented as sort of nodes in graphs and are activated through a mechanism of "spreading activation", implemented through a marker passing algorithm, allowing the propagation of information through the network to determine the strength of the relationships between concepts. In this setting, the higher the activation of a node in the network, the more contextually relevant that node/concept was assumed to be for the task in focus. Interestingly enough, the research on Semantic Networks paved the way for both the development of the first graph-like, knowledge-based systems and formalisms (which make use of so-called *symbolic* representations) as well as the improvement of the so-called *connectionist* or *sub-symbolic* systems, since the

4 As we will see in more detail in the following sections, the ingredients required for the execution of this kind of heuristic strategy – essentially based on a "search space" approach to problem solving – explicitly supported the so-called "symbolic approach" for the study, analysis, execution, and replication of intelligent behaviour in artificial systems.

5 Herbert Simon is arguably one of the most important scientists of the last century. His influence, indeed, went well beyond his original training in cognitive psychology. Simon was awarded a Nobel Prize in Economics for his studies on "bounded rationality", which showed – differing from the classical decision models of the time – how humans are not optimal decision makers. This field of study has led to the development of an entirely new discipline that is nowadays known as "behavioural economics". In addition, he was one of the founding fathers and main protagonist of the field of AI; along with people like Marvin Minsky, John McCarthy, Allen Newell, Nathaniel Rochester, and many others, he was an active participant in the Dartmouth Workshop. As a result of his "bounded rationality" theory in decision making, he was, one of the first scholars to point out, in both cognitive psychology and AI, the role played by heuristics as decisional shortcuts to solve complex problems. The application of the heuristic approach in the context of AI was one of the reasons behind him winning, in 1975, the Turing Award, together with Allen Newell. The particular meanings attributed to the term "heuristics" in the AI research, will be explained later in this chapter.

concept of "spreading activation" has been very influential in the context of the "connectionist" investigations (see Cordeschi, 2002: 235, on this point). Before proceeding further with our examples of early cognitively inspired AI systems, it is necessary to briefly introduce the above-mentioned basic notions of "symbolic representations" (and paradigm) and "connectionist or sub-symbolic representations" (and paradigm), since they have been, and still are, really crucial modelling methods in both the past and present AI and cognitive modelling communities. In particular, the notion of "symbolic representation" constitutes a core assumption of the so-called "symbolic paradigm" in AI and cognitive science (which will be better clarified in more detail later in the book). In short, according to this view, intelligence in natural and artificial systems is associated with the capability of storing and manipulating the information in terms of abstract "symbols" (representing, in many cases, some mental proxy associated with external physical objects) and on the capability of executing mental operations and calculations over such symbols. This view was (is) severely criticized by the so-called "connectionist or sub-symbolic paradigm", according to which the organization of the "mental content" in natural and artificial systems is not based on any symbolic structure but is, on the other hand, (1) distributed in nature and (2) based on parallel models of computations (these are the two core assumptions of the "connectionist representations"), in a way that is more similar to the biological organization and processing mechanisms of neurons and synapses in our brain. From a modelling perspective, this approach has led to the development of the Artificial Neural Networks, or ANNs (partially inspired by the biological neural structure of our brain), and self-organizing systems. We will discuss later the impact of "neural" or brain-inspired methods in early (and modern) AI research.[6] For the moment it is probably worth mentioning that, from a historical point of view, the "symbolic paradigm" represented the mainstream assumption in the context of both early AI and cognitive modelling research.

A confirmation of what was just discussed is provided by the next example of a cognitively inspired AI framework, which we are going to investigate: the notion of *Frames* (still a symbolic representational framework) operated by Marvin Minsky almost a decade after Quillian's proposal (Minsky, 1975). With this proposal, Minsky intended to attack another well-known "symbolic approach"

---

6 For the sake of completeness, it is also worth mentioning that within the cognitive modelling and AI communities another paradigm has been historically proposed relying on so-called "analog" or "diagrammatic" representations. In particular, according to the supporters of this school of thought, mental representations take the form of "pictures" in the mind. There are many different examples of analog representations proposed, one of the most famous corresponding to the "mental models" by Johnson-Laird (1983, 2006). A general underlying assumption of this class of representation is that "spatial cognition" abilities (represented via these "picture-like" schemas) are a core aspect of natural cognitive systems from which other intelligent mechanisms emerge (e.g., the mental models by Johnson Laird have been notoriously proposed to model different types of inferences).

developed back then: the "logicist"[7] position à la McCarthy for the representation of knowledge in artificial systems. In particular, Minsky argued that such a proposal was not able to deal with the flexibility of the commonsense reasoning that is so evident in human beings. Frames, on the other hand, were proposed for endowing AI systems with commonsense knowledge (including *default* knowledge) about the external world.[8] The type of knowledge organization proposed in the Frames enabled the first AI systems to extend their automated reasoning abilities from classical deduction to more complicated forms of commonsense and defeasible reasoning (going from induction to abduction). In this case, the idea of the Frames was directly inspired by the work of the psychologist Eleanor Rosch (Rosch, 1975) about the organization of conceptual information in humans known as the "prototype theory"[9] as well as by the memory "schemas" proposed by the cognitive psychologist Bartlett (Bartlett, 1958). A simple example and use case, done by Minsky himself, of a frame data structure is the following: let us imagine opening a door inside a house we are not familiar with. In this case, we typically expect to find a room that more or less is characterized by features that we have already seen in other rooms we have been in. Such features are referred to as a body of knowledge organized in the form of prototypes (i.e., the typical room). The data structures that reflect this flexible way of using knowledge, which is typical of human beings, can be described as "frame systems". Therefore, the "room frame" is a characterized by different types of information that includes – listed in appropriate "slots" – the typical features of a room, such as a certain number of doors, walls, windows, and so on. There could be various kinds of rooms – dining rooms, bedrooms, etc. – each constituting, in turn, a frame with more specific features, again listed in appropriate slots. This kind of representation also allows for individual differences in conceptualization; e.g., Francesca's dining room might be quite different from Paola's in various details, but it will always be part of one and the same kind of room frame. The proposal of the frames as data structures for commonsense reasoning was not

---

7 A brief overview of the logical approaches proposed in the 1970s to deal with commonsense reasoning (e.g., circumscription, fuzzy logic, etc.) is sketched out in the next chapter of the book. At this point, it is important to point out that the logicist tradition was (is) deeply rooted in the symbolic representation assumption, briefly elaborated on above and further detailed in the next section of this chapter.

8 As indicated elsewhere, "all the forms of commonsense reasoning can be seen as a bounded rationality phenomenon since they represent a plethora of shortcuts allowing us (i.e., "bounded-rational" agents) to make decisions in an environment with incomplete and uncertain information" (Lieto, 2020: 56).

9 According to the prototype theory posited by Rosch, concepts are organised in our mind as "prototypes" (i.e., in terms of typical representative elements of that category) and such an organization explains many types of so-called "typicality effects" (i.e., of commonsense inferences) that we naturally perform in our everyday reasoning. We will return on this specific aspect later and more extensively in the book (particularly in Chapter 4), since commonsense reasoning represents one of the main areas of possible convergence between Cognitive Science and AI.

completely successful from a computational point of view (since frame systems did not scale well) but was very influential for the development of research in the context of commonsense reasoning.

In those years, a proposal very much aligned with Minsky's was put forth by Roger Schank and his "conceptual dependency" theory (Schank, 1972). Schank aimed at explaining natural-language understanding phenomena via psychologically plausible computational processes. He proposed identifying a small set of "semantic primitives", the use of which would have made it possible to construct the representation of meaning for any English verb. In his original programs, a sentence was analyzed by making explicit its representation in terms of semantic primitives. Such primitives were considered common to all natural languages and constituted a sort of interlingua. This interlingua was then used to build the first machine translation systems (e.g., MARGIE, see Shank & Nash-Webber, 1975). When Schank passed from constructing programs translating single sentences to ones aimed at translating entire stories, he realized that it was necessary to take commonsense into account. In this respect, a relevant problem concerned the knowledge needed to derive meaningful inferences from the union of different sentences in a story, so as to make explicit the implicit beliefs and expectations assumed in the context of a story. To tackle this and other problems, Schank and Abelson (1977) endowed their program – SAM (Script Applier Mechanism) – with "scripts". Scripts are a data structure for representing knowledge of common sequences of events (e.g., the sequence of events used to go out for dinner) and are used in natural-language processing systems as way to enable intelligent answers to questions about simple stories. A classic example used to explain the notion of a "script" (which is also tightly connected with the notion of a "Frame") is the so called "restaurant situation". Let us consider a situation of an agent going out to a restaurant for dinner. A script representing the restaurant situation is a data structure that would record the typical events associated with this scenario; e.g., entering the restaurant, asking for a table, sitting down, consulting a menu, eating the food, paying the check, etc. This kind of representational structure enabled early AI systems to answer questions about simple stories. For example, let us consider a story like this: "Mary went to a restaurant and ordered salmon. When she was paying, she noticed that she was late for her next appointment." In this case, computerized systems were able to answer a question such as, "Did Mary eat dinner last night?" in a positive way (as we do). It is worth noticing that this information is not explicitly provided in the story. Answering these types of questions is possible through the use of a "script" of the restaurant situation.

The capability of understanding natural-language instructions was also a crucial feature of Terry Winograd's famous robotic system known as SHRDLU (named for the alphabetic symbols composing a row of keyboards in that era). In SHRDLU (Winograd, 1972), interactions with humans focused on a simulated blocks world that humans could view on a graphics display and to which the system had direct access. Users drove the conversation via written text by typing sentences, including commands like, "Find a block that is taller than the one you are holding and put it into the box" and "Is there anything that is bigger than every pyramid but not as wide as the thing that supports it?". As reported in Langley (2017),

> These inputs required not only the ability to parse quite complex structures and extract their meanings but also to draw inferences about relationships and execute multistep activities. The innovative system handled simple anaphora, disambiguated word senses, and had basic memory for its previous interactions.

SHRDLU was, therefore, an important advancement because it integrated sentence level understanding, reasoning about domain content, execution of multistep activities, and natural interaction with human users. At that time, there was no other artificial system able to show the same range of capabilities, and it offered a proof of concept that such an integrated intelligent system was possible. This accomplishment, of course, relied on some important simplifications: SHRDLU operated in a narrow and well-defined domain and had complete access to the entire state of the simulated environment. Nevertheless, it was an impressive achievement, which fostered further work on intelligent agents. To a certain extent, the integrated abilities exhibited by SHRDLU were the inspiration also for the subsequent work of Allen Newell and his colleagues at Carnegie Mellon University, concerning the development of the first integrated cognitive architecture for general intelligence: SOAR (Newell, Laird, & Rosenbloom, 1982).[10]

At the very time that SOAR was first being developed (by now we were already in the mid-1980s), another relevant proposal in the context of cognitively inspired AI was made, once again, by Marvin Minsky, who introduced the evocative idea of the "Society of Mind" (Minsky, 1986, 2007) as a way to conceptualize, analyze, and design intelligent behaviour. This idea relies on the importance of considering, in natural and artificial agents, problem-solving activities "in layers" of interconnected micro-faculties (i.e., as a "society" of processes). In particular, Minsky suggested that the capability of dealing with commonsense knowledge[11] is the grounding element of these layers of growing thinking capabilities. Such an approach has been historically impactful – not from an engineering perspective (since much more detail would have been needed in the Minsky proposal to specify how the processes can and should interact in an

---

10 On the role of cognitive architectures for general intelligent systems we remind to (Lieto et al., 2018). We will return to SOAR and to cognitive architectures over the course of the book. In addition to the SHRDLU influence, SOAR was heavily inspired by the heuristic search mechanisms already developed in the GPS system.

11 Commonsense knowledge is acquired, according to the Minsky proposal, via "instinctive" or "learned" reactions, and is then processed towards the higher hierarchies of "deliberative", "reflective", "self-reflective", and "self-conscious" thinking at the level of both individual and social context.

efficient computer implementation) – but mainly for the idea of considering, from a methodological and modelling perspective, the classical problem-solving activity (which was already modelled in systems like GPS or SOAR) through this sort of layered conceptual view involving a multistep reasoning process. As we will see in the following sections, this layered approach influenced, under completely different assumptions, another protagonist of the AI story from the previous century: Rodney Brooks.[12]

This list of examples of early cognitively inspired AI systems reviewed so far is, of course, not exhaustive. However, all these early systems shared a common "view" about the study of intelligence in artificial systems. More precisely, all these systems adhere – at different levels – to the so-called "cognitivist tradition"[13] of AI, also known as GOFAI (Good Old Fashioned AI).

Such early view is successfully synthesized by Pat Langley (Langley, 2012), who said, "(Early) AI aimed at understanding and reproducing in computational systems the full range of intelligent behaviour observed by humans" (Langley, 2012).

Langley identifies the following set of features that characterize the early AI period and the main cognitivist modelling assumptions:

- the role of symbolic representations as a building block upon which operate a set of manipulation operations to let intelligent behaviour emerge;
- the importance of a general cognitively inspired approach to the study of the mind and intelligence (what Pat Langley calls a "system view");
- the main focus on the so-called "high level cognition" (the systems for natural language processing,[14] for example, underwent a big development in this early period);
- the adoption of heuristics (we will return on this concept later) as a method for problem solving;
- the intrinsic interdisciplinary and exploratory nature of the research.

We will analyze in more details these aspects of the cognitivist tradition (and its differences from emergentist perspectives) in the next few sections of the chapter.

---

12 Rodney Brooks is a roboticist and was previously an MIT Professor. He is the creator of "Herbert" the robot, the first mobile robot able to exhibit interesting reactive behaviours without any central controlled activity. For more details about the particular layered architecture proposed by Brooks, known as "Subsumption Architecture", we refer the reader to the next section.

13 As will be clarified in the following pages, the "cognitivist" tradition is deeply rooted in the so-called "symbolic paradigm" and was the dominant perspective during the early days of AI research. Cognitivist assumptions differ from those of the "emergentist" approaches, which are, on the other hand, rooted in the notions of bottom-up self-organisation (see Vernon, 2014).

14 A typical example of the systems developed in this period is Eliza (Weizenbaum, 1966), one of the first conversational agents (nowadays called "chatbots"), created to converse with a human being, simulating, at least up to a certain extent, the behaviour of a psychotherapist.

However, from a historical perspective, it is worth mentioning that this approach to the study of the artificial did not come out *ex-abrupto*. It borrowed its original inspiration, even if grounded on different assumptions, from the methodological apparatus developed by scholars in cybernetics (Cordeschi, 1991). The origins of cybernetics, in fact, are usually traced back to the middle of the 1940s, with the release of the 1948 book by Norbert Wiener entitled *Cybernetics: Or Control and Communication in the Animal and the Machine*. An underlying idea of cybernetics was one about building mechanical models to simulate the adaptive behaviour of natural systems. As indicated in Cordeschi (Cordeschi, 2002): "The fundamental insight of cybernetics was in the proposal of a unified study of organisms and machines". In this perspective, the computational simulation of biological processes was assumed to play a central epistemological role in the development and refinement of theories about the elements characterizing the nature of intelligent behaviour in natural and artificial systems. Such kind of simulative approach, as mentioned, was inherited by the early AI research that used computer programs to reproduce performances, which, if observed in human beings, would be regarded as "intelligent". The adoption of such a perspective was crucial in AI, for the development of both intelligent solutions inspired by human processes and heuristics (Newell & Simon, 1976; Gigerenzer & Todd, 1999) and for the realization of computational models of cognition built with the aim of providing a deeper understanding of human thinking, as originally suggested in the manifesto of Information Processing Psychology (IPP) (Newell & Simon, 1972). These two sides of the cognitivist tradition are nowadays still alive. They correspond, roughly, to the research areas known as "cognitively inspired AI" (or "cognitive systems") and "cognitive modelling" (or "computational cognitive science"), respectively.

Heuristics and AI eras

The notion of heuristics deserves, in this historical account, special attention. Usually, this term, derived from the Greek word "eureka", indicates a non-optimal problem-solving procedure adopting particular "shortcuts" to reach a given goal. This term has been ascribed two different meanings since the times of the first AI research. In its first sense, the term refers to the most detailed simulation possible of human cognitive processes, and it characterized the above-mentioned IPP, introduced by Newell and Simon. In this view, a computer program was considered to be a model providing a test of the hypothesis that the mind is an information-processing system. More precisely, "the program was considered to be a highly specific behavioral theory, concerning the behavior of an individual human problem-solver: a microtheory" (Cordeschi, 2002: 182).[15]

---

15 In this view, the general theory of human information-processing was assumed to be derivable from a body of qualitative generalizations coming from the study of individual simulative programs, or microtheories.

In another sense, the term refers to the possibility of obtaining the most efficient (and efficacious) performance possible from computer programs, by allowing also for typically non-human procedures, such as those where the computer can excel. Before the introduction of the term "heuristics" in AI – operated by Newell, Shaw, and Simon – there were already algorithmic procedures available, which might have been defined as heuristic in the second of these senses and which had already been tried out experimentally. The first among them were the procedures that allowed the program developed by Arthur Samuel to play checkers despite the combinatory explosion of moves (Samuel, 1959).

The fact that these two tendencies, reflected in the double meaning of the term "heuristic", coexisted in AI was immediately clear. As reported in Cordeschi (2002: 190), in 1961, while discussing a presentation of GPS given by Simon during a seminar at MIT, Minsky drew a distinction in AI research between those who were willing to use "non-human techniques" in constructing intelligent programs and those, like the Carnegie-Mellon group, who were interested in simulating human cognitive processes.[16] This distinction is crucial, since it outlines the emergence of different research agendas that were already present at that time. In the following decades these early distinctions became deeper and determined the difference between "Nature-" or "Human-inspired" approaches to the development of artificial systems versus "Machine-oriented" approaches to the solution of a given problem.

Modelling paradigms and AI eras: cognitivist and emergentist perspectives

As briefly illustrated in the previous sections, the early days of AI were mainly characterized by the "cognitivist" assumption that intelligent activity in both living and artificial systems was possible due to the capability of encoding knowledge about the external world via "internal" abstract symbolic representations, directly corresponding to elements of the reality. In this setting, intelligent behaviour (e.g., in language, vision, planning, etc.) was viewed as the expression of operations carried out on such symbols and the motto of this early phase (also known as "cognitivism", see e.g., Vernon, 2014) was synthesized by the expression "cognition is computation". Here, the word "computation" was intended to mean the capability of manipulating such symbolic structures. The theoretical reference framework that inspired such an assumption, in both cognitive psychology and artificial intelligence, was the so-called "Physical Symbol System

---

16 As reported in Cordeschi (2002), Minsky emphasized that these two tendencies were distinguished "in methods and goals" from a third tendency, which "has a physiological orientation and alleges to be based on an imitation of the brain," i.e., neural net and self-organizing system approaches. We will discuss later in this book the "neural" or brain-inspired methods in early (and modern) AI research. As anticipated, such approaches belong to the so-called "connectionist agenda".

Hypothesis" (PSSH), introduced by Newell and Simon (1976). According to this theory, intelligent beings are physical symbol systems. In this framework, symbolic representations were not only a denotational means for referring to entities of the external world but also a means for denoting other internal symbolic structures (thus allowing to hypothesise an internal information processing mechanism able to overcome the classical Input-Output direct mapping assumed by the *behaviourist tradition*[17]). In this view, symbolic systems are assumed to be realizable by means of different "hardware" (e.g., a Von Neumann architecture or a natural brain[18]) and symbolic processing is considered a necessary and sufficient condition for intelligent behaviour. In particular, the apparatus of such a hypothesis assumes that an intelligent agent should be equipped with the following elements (Newell, 1990):

- Memory Systems (to contain the symbolic information)
- Symbols (to provide a pattern to match or index other symbols)
- Operations (to manipulate symbols)
- Interpretations (to allow symbols to specify operations)
- Symbolic Capacities for
  - Compositionality
  - Interpretability

With respect to what was mentioned earlier about the "symbolic paradigm", some additional clarifications are needed to fully grasp what concerns both the "Symbols" and the "Compositionality" requirements identified by Newell in the above mentioned list.

17 Behaviourism (in this context we are referring to so-called "methodological behaviourism", which is different from "philosophical behaviourism") is a methodological approach to the study of behaviour in natural systems, born at the beginning of last century, and based on the observable analysis of the responses (e.g., the produced output) to certain stimuli (the input) manipulated via different types of reinforcement (this is also known as "operant conditioning"). Watson (1913), one of the founders of this approach, defined psychology as "a purely objective experimental branch of natural science" and its program as the "prediction and control of behavior". As a consequence of this radical view, behaviourists did not consider/analyze the internal mechanisms driving a given behaviour (provided certain stimuli). The now-famous experiments done by the Russian physiologist and Nobel Prize winner Ivan Pavlov about the conditioned reflex of dogs and their automatic stimulus-response behaviour (where the stimulus was constituted by a "ringing bell" that the dogs had learn to associate to the arrival of food, and the response to the salivation caused by the bell ringing) was an important landmark in this tradition (as was his other work about so-called "classical conditioning"). This approach, was severely criticised by the cognitivist tradition in psychology, the "computationalist" view in the philosophy of mind, and Information Processing Psychology, which, on the other hand, assumed the presence of internal information processing mechanisms as driving forces leading to a manifest behaviour.

18 This claimed "interchangeability" means that, in this framework, the physical instantiation (i.e., the "hardware") *per se* is not important since the intelligent behaviour emerging via symbol manipulation is assumed to be independent of the particular form of the instantiation.

For what concerns the "symbols", as mentioned, the PSSH assumes that such abstract structures can refer to and be combined with (as is evident more clearly in the figure 1.1 below) other internal symbols and processes.

This possibility is important in light of the "compositionality" requirement. Compositionality is an important feature of symbolic systems and is also considered an irrevocable trait of human cognition. In a compositional system of representation, it is possible to distinguish between a set of primitive, or atomic, symbols and a set of complex symbols. Complex symbols are generated from primitive symbols through the application of suitable recursive syntactic rules: generally, a potentially infinite set of complex symbols can be generated from a finite set of primitive symbols. The meaning of complex symbols can be determined starting from the meaning of primitive symbols, using recursive semantic rules that work in parallel with syntactic composition rules. In the context of classical cognitive science, it is often assumed that mental representations are indeed compositional. A clear and explicit formulation of this assumption was proposed by Fodor and Pylyshyn (Fodor & Pylyshyn, 1988). They claim that the compositionality of mental representations is mandatory to explain fundamental cognitive phenomena (i.e., the generative and systematic character of human cognition) and they also show how the contrasting neural, distributed representations encoded in artificial neural networks are not compositional.[19]

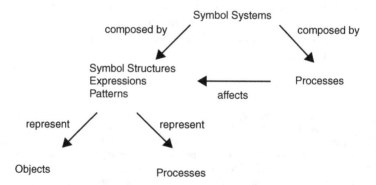

FIGURE 1.1 Overview of the internal dynamics of physical symbol systems (adapted from Vernon, 2014).

19 It is worth noting that, while standard compositionality is easily handled by symbolic system, "commonsense compositionally" (i.e., one involving typicality-based reasoning à la Rosch) has always been a problematic aspect to model. This problem is paradigmatically represented by the so called PET FISH problem: if we consider this concept, in its prototypical characterisation, as the result of the composition of the prototypical representations of the concepts "PET" and "FISH", we soon realise that the prototype of pet fish cannot result from the composition of the "PET" and "FISH". A typical pet – indeed – is furry and warm, a typical fish is greyish, but a typical pet fish is neither furry and warm nor greyish (typically, it is red). The pet fish phenomenon is a classic example of the difficulty to deal with when building formalisms and systems aiming at imitating this compositional human ability. Nowadays, a proposal to deal with the

Given this state of affairs, then, solving a problem for a physical symbol system means being able to perform a Heuristic Search within a problem space represented by symbolic structures. Here, in fact, the intelligent behaviour is assumed to emerge by generating and progressively modifying symbol structures until a solution structure (e.g., a goal) is reached. This overall assumption is known as the Heuristic Search Hypothesis[20] and, as it is probably evident to the readers, some of the above-mentioned early systems like GPS (as well as the formalisms like the Semantic Networks and, as we will see, SOAR as well) are heavily built upon the PSSH and its Heuristic Search corollary.

Parallel to these "symbolic" developments, a radically different modelling approach based on neuron-like "subsymbolic" or "connectionist" computations (e.g., Grossberg, 1976; McClelland, 2010) was being explored. Proponents of this approach (one of the most successful in the so-called "emergentist" field[21]) maintain that many classic types of structured knowledge, such as graphs, grammars, rules, objects, structural descriptions, programs, etc., can be useful yet misleading metaphors for characterizing "thought" in both natural and artificial systems. In particular, these structures are seen as epiphenomenal rather than real, emergent properties of more fundamental sub-symbolic cognitive processes (McClelland, 2010) (Figure 1.1).

In general, in contrast to the symbolic paradigm, the knowledge in these neural networks is distributed across a collection of units rather than localized as in symbolic data structures. The central idea of such models, in fact, is that a large number of simple computational units can achieve intelligent behaviour when networked together. This insight applies equally to neurons in biological nervous systems and to hidden units in computational models. The representations and

---

problem of commonsense compositionality in symbolic systems was proposed in Lieto and Pozzato (2020) and applied to both cognitive modelling problems (e.g., the PET FISH) and in the context of computational creativity applications. Nonetheless, modelling commonsense reasoning (including commonsense compositionality) in a human-like fashion and with human-level performances remains an open problem in the context of symbolic systems.

20 The Heuristic search hypothesis has been very influential in AI since many algorithms (e.g., from the "hill climbing" to the "beam search" to the notorious A* algorithm) that have been developed to improve the efficiency of finding optimal or suboptimal paths in problems represented as a graph-like structure have been developed by starting from this hypothesis. For an introduction to these classical algorithms, we refer the reader to introductory books on AI (see e.g., Russell & Norvig, 2002). One of the first successful and convincing implementations of such "search-based" approaches (e.g., the A* algorithm) was in the robot Shakey, developed in 1966 by Nilsson and colleagues (see Hart et al., 1968; Nilsson, 1971; Fikes et al., 1972).

21 The expression "emergentist approaches" is determined by the fact that the class of modelling frameworks of this tradition assume that the information to be processed is learned from the environment in a bottom-up way and intelligent behaviour (if any) is assumed to be an emergent property coming from this interaction. Within emergentist frameworks we can include dynamical systems (using differential equations to model the dynamic of a system and its change over time, caused by the interaction with the environment) and enactive approaches (usually employing both connectionist and dynamical frameworks and assuming embodied agents). We refer to Vernon (2014, Chapter 2), for an introduction to such frameworks.

algorithms used by this approach, therefore, were (and are) more directly inspired by neuroscience rather than psychology. As a consequence, differing from the PSSH, in this modelling framework (and in general all the so-called emergentist modelling frameworks) the "physical hardware" (e.g., the body) instantiating the actual computation is assumed to play an important role.

From a historical perspective, the connectionist movement took inspiration from the functional models of nervous cells, introduced in the pioneering work by Warren McCulloch and Walter Pitts (developed during the pre-cybernetic period and heavily influencing cybernetic research), showing how every "net" of formal neurons – if furnished with a tape and suitable input, output, and scanning systems – is equivalent to a Turing machine[22] (McCulloch & Pitts, 1943). Such initial insights were later enriched by research from Donald Hebb (Hebb, 1948) about the learning processes in the nervous system[23] and further studies of learning and classification processes in networks, à la McCullock and Pitts, lead to the development of the first artificial neural network (ANN) known as Perceptron (developed by Rosenblatt in 1958).[24]

After these pioneering works, during the 1960s, research on neural nets seemed to take a step back once a notorious book by Minsky and Papert (1969) showed the limitations of the then-existent Perceptron in discriminating very simple visual stimuli. Despite such limitations, however, various researchers continued to work on this framework and the "renascence of neural nets", that took place in the 1980s, happened in ground that was still fertile. Nevertheless, "this renascence was marked by at least two crucial events, accompanied by the development in those years of computers with great computing power, allowing them to simulate neural nets of increasing complexity" (Cordeschi, 2002: 213). In particular, in 1982, John Hopfield proved that symmetrical neural nets necessarily evolve towards steady states – then interpreted as attractors in the dynamic system theory – and that they can function as associative memories (Hopfield, 1982). In 1985, James MacLelland, David Rumelhart, and their collaborators introduced the approach known as parallel distributed processing (PDP) of information by starting a number of investigations on natural language acquisition by emphasizing the role of artificial neural networks and of parallel computation

---

22 In 1936, Turing introduced the abstract computing machine bearing his name and explicitly construed a universal machine that could simulate, with appropriate encoding, any computation carried out by any Turing machine (including, of course, the universal one) (Turing, 1936–37).

23 Roughly speaking, so-called "Hebbian learning" consists of the evidence that when the axon of a given cell A is near enough to excite a cell B and repeatedly or persistently takes part in firing it, this kind of associative connection A→B leaves a trace in the nervous system that learns this simple associative rule.

24 The Perceptron was one of the first neural network architectures. This simple form of neural network consists of a first layer, corresponding to the sensory system (an analog for a retina), which is randomly connected to one or more elements in a second layer of nodes: the association system. The latter consists of association cells, or A-units, whose output is a function of the input signal.

in the study of cognitive phenomena. They showed how a learning algorithm based on error correction, known as "backpropagation",[25] made it possible to overcome the main limitations of neural nets described by Minsky and Papert (Rumelhart, McClelland, & the PDP Research Group, 1986).[26] Back then, the achieved results had a strong echo since they were also considered the first example countering the predominant (in both linguistics and AI) Chomskian view of language processing, which took moves from the book "Syntactic Structures" (Chomsky, 1957), declaring the primacy of syntax and grammars. Since these pioneering works, connectionist systems have been widely adopted in a variety of applications in both the cognitive modelling and AI communities. Connectionist systems (and emergent systems in general) have been important in the AI landscape since they have provided more suitable solutions (with respect to the symbolic approach) able to deal with the environment and with the processing of the perceptual aspects of sensory input. In particular, they have fought the tendency of (early) symbolic AI to consider, in an isolated way, perceptual systems, motor systems, and high-level cognitive functions etc.[27] On the other hand, they have targeted the close interaction between the "mind" (natural or artificial), the body (i.e., the "hardware"), and environment.[28] This has led, in some cases, to radical

25 The backpropagation rule intervenes to change the weights of the connections between the hidden units, going backward from the error, which is calculated at the output units. Rosenblatt had anticipated the formulation of various aspects of this rule that, however, was fully formalised by Geff Hinton, winner of the Turing Award Prize in 2019 for, among the other things, the invention of the backpropagation algorithm.

26 The work and its assumptions were not free from criticisms. See, for example, Pinker and Prince (1988) and the subsequent debate that dominated the late 1980s and 1990s.

27 This tendency was, in a later period, contrasted also within the cognitivist/symbolic approach by Allen Newell. While Simon, in fact, continued his development of "microtheories" or "middle-range" theories (see Cordeschi, 2002) by focusing on the refinement of the analysis of verbal protocol, Newell didn't consider the construction of single simulative microtheories a sufficient means to enable the generalisation of "unifying" theories of cognition (the original goal of Information Processing Psychology). Therefore, diverging from Simon, he proposed building simulative programs independent from single cognitive tasks and able to include invariant structures of human cognition. In this way, he started the enterprise of studying and developing integrated and multi-tasking intelligence via cognitive architectures that would have led to the development of the SOAR system.

28 It is worth noticing, however, that in classic "cognitivist" tradition as well the importance of the environment in the deployment of intelligent behaviour was somehow recognised. Herbert Simon, in fact, in his lecture series on "The sciences of the artificial" (later published as a famous book with the same title), introduced the so-called "Ant metaphor", which would later come to be known as "Simon's Ant metaphor" and which can be described as follows: "An ant, viewed as a behaving system, is quite simple. The apparent complexity of its behaviour over time is largely a reflection of the complexity of the environment in which it finds itself". Simon then applies this consideration to human beings by suggesting that the apparent complexity of human behaviour is also largely a reflection of the complexity of the environment in which we live. Therefore he suggests that the environment should play an important role in building simulative models of cognition since "the behaviour takes on the shape of the task environment". Despite these relevant insights, however, early AI systems assuming the PSSH did not succeed in integrating such aspects in their models and were severely criticized by proponents of the

assumptions that have proposed the complete elimination of the notion of "representation" (intended in the cognitivist/symbolic sense) from the vocabulary of the cognitive and artificial sciences. This movement was led by the roboticist Rodney Brooks through the proposal of the so-called "Subsumption Architecture" (Brooks, 1986, 1991). This proposal consists of a layered, decentralized, robotic control architecture that does not make any use of internal representation of the world (i.e., the motto of this view is "use the world as a model"), where the relevant parts of the control system interact and activate each other through sensing the world. Subsumption architecture has been very influential from an engineering point of view since a vast variety of effective, implemented robotic systems use it.[29] It is based on the so-called "creature hypothesis", according to which the most important part in the design of an intelligent artificial system can be reduced to the difficulty of building a machine that act as smart as an insect. In other words, the underlying assumption of such a hypothesis is that once the perceptual/reactive part of a "creature" (natural or artificial) is built, then building the rest of the intelligence features is an easy task to achieve. The figure 1.2 below shows the characteristics of this kind of architecture. Each layer, programmed by using finite state machines of problem solving was assumed to deal with specific tasks (e.g., the task of avoiding obstacles, wandering, seeking, etc.) and higher levels of the hierarchy subsume the actions of lower levels. The design of successive task-achieving layers is stopped once the overall desired task is achieved (Figure 1.2).

Such radical proposal, however, has also shown significant limitations. In fact, even if they lead, through the development of innovative architectures for decentralized action control, to the ability of acting in non-structured environments in real time, these systems nevertheless showed their limitations when asked to deal with more high-level cognitive tasks, such as planning, reasoning, multi-agent coordination, and so on. Such tasks, on the other hand, were dealt with in a more satisfactory way via the symbolic approach, thus suggesting the practical utility of the notion of "representation".

The classical move, in this case, was the adoption of hybrid approaches trying to connect low-level and high-level faculties by integrating neural and symbolic approaches. Investigations of the integration between "symbolic" and "subsymbolic" in AI have coexisted during recent decades, but despite the realization of

---

"emergentist" paradigms. Emergentist modelling approaches, in fact, have proven to be more efficacious in modelling the environment and its intervention in the emergence of intelligent behaviour.

29 The first implementation of such an architecture was executed in robots like "Allen" and "Herbert", developed by Brooks and his group at MIT in the late 1980s. In particular, Herbert, a soda-can collecting robot, was able to exhibit the following capabilities (uncommon at that time): moving around in a real environment without running into obstacles; detecting soda cans using a camera and a laser; using an arm that could extend, sense, and evaluate whether or not to pick up the soda can, etc. Nowadays, Subsumption Architecture is employed in the most successful robotic platform so far: the Roomba robot!

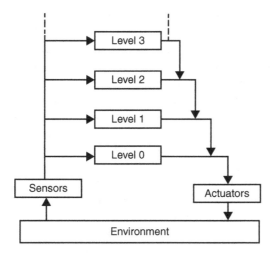

FIGURE 1.2 Brooks' Subsumption Architecture (adapted from Brooks, 1999).

many hybrid systems, a general solution to the problem of the *ad-hoc* integration of such heterogeneous components does not yet exist. In particular, connectionist models have continued to achieve the best results in handling activities like pattern recognition and classification or associative learning. They have failed, however, in handling higher cognitive functions, like complex inference-based reasoning, which are better modelled by symbolic approaches.[30] A well-known problem of these connectionist representations, for example, concerns the difficulty of implementing compositionality in neural networks (Fodor & Pylyshyn, 1988). Finally, another classical problem of artificial neural networks is represented by their "opacity": a neural network behaves as a sort of "black box" and specific interpretation for the operation of its units and weights is far from trivial. Despite such foundational problems, today neural networks are used in a variety of fields that range from machine vision to natural language processing to autonomous cars, due to the success of the new generation of deep learning architectures. On the other hand, symbolic approaches also suffer from a number of problems, other than the above-mentioned ones of dealing with commonsense reasoning and commonsense compositionality; these range from the "frame problem" (McCarthy & Hayes, 1969) to the "symbol grounding" one (Harnad, 1990). In short, the frame problem consists of a difficulty in formally

---

30 The novel generation of connectionist models based on deep learning have also recently gained attention for the results obtained in tasks like automated machine translation (Jean et al., 2015). However, this success in language based tasks seems to be mainly obtained because that task has been treated as a machine vision task, where the structure (i.e., the patterns) of a source language had to be mapped and compared with the one of a target language. Despite these new achievements, deep learning language models still provide poor results, compared to other approaches, in high-level cognitive tasks, ranging from Question Answering and Narrative/Story Comprehension to Commonsense Reasoning.

representing, in logic-based representational languages, changes in an environment in which an agent (e.g., a robot) has to solve some tasks without having to explicitly resort to an enormous number of axioms to also exclude a number of intuitively obvious – for humans – non-effects. For example, if a robot places a cup on a table, it is necessary not only specify that the cup is now on the table, but also that the light remains on, that the table is still in the same place, that the robot is still in the same room, etc. The symbol grounding issue, on the other hand, concerns the problem of how to obtain the grounding between symbolic representations and the corresponding entities that they denote in the external world. This is notoriously hard for symbolic systems and is alleviated in connectionist systems, since the data they directly take in input (e.g., images, signals, etc.) are closer to the perceptual "real world" sensory data. Summing up: the last 65 years of applied research have shown that both the main modelling approaches developed in the context of cognitive modelling and AI communities have different strengths and limitations. In any case they are not able to account, if considered in isolation, for all aspects of cognitive faculties.

Death and rebirth of a collaboration

As showed in the previous sections, AI pioneers were explicitly inspired by research on human cognition, and the cognitive approach was considered – without any doubt – to be the best strategy to pursue, so as to build intelligent machines (see Lake et al., 2017). Schank (1972), in the journal *Cognitive Psychology*, declared, "We hope to be able to build a program that can learn, as a child does, how to do what we have described in this paper instead of being spoon-fed the tremendous information necessary". A similar sentiment was expressed by Minsky (1975):

> I draw no boundary between a theory of human thinking and a scheme for making an intelligent machine; no purpose would be served by separating these today since neither domain has theories good enough to explain or to produce enough mental capacity.

This initial (excessive) enthusiasm, however, started to vanish (a fierce critique on the over-the-top optimism of that period was given by Hubert Dreyfus, 1972) and, after the first few decades of pioneering collaborations, starting from the mid-1980s, AI and the new-born interdisciplinary field of Cognitive Science started to produce several sub-fields, each with its own goals, methods, and evaluation criteria. On one hand, this divorce from considering human or nature-inspired heuristics has led AI to achieving remarkable results in a variety of specific fields (by focusing on quantitative results and metrics of performance, and on a machine-oriented approach to the intelligent behaviour). On the other hand, however, it has significantly inhibited cross-field collaborations and research efforts targeted at investigating a more general picture of what natural and artificial intelligence is, and how intelligent artefacts can be designed by taking into account the insights coming from human cognition.

In the last few years, however, the cognitive approach to AI has gained renewed consideration, both from academia and the industry, in wide research areas such as Knowledge Representation and Reasoning, Robotics, Machine Learning, Bio-Inspired Cognitive Computing, Computational Creativity, and other research fields that aspire to human-level intelligence. Nowadays, in fact, artificial systems endowed with human-like and human-level intelligence (McCarthy, 2007) are still far from being achieved and, using the words of Aaron Sloman, "the gap between natural and artificial intelligence is still enormous" (Sloman, 2014). This sort of "cognitive renaissance" of AI still considers the "cognition in the loop" approach as a useful one to detect and unveil novel and hidden aspects of cognitive theories by building properly designed computational models of cognition, which are useful to progress towards a deeper understanding of the foundational roots of intelligence (both in natural and artificial systems).

2

COGNITIVE AND MACHINE-ORIENTED APPROACHES TO INTELLIGENCE IN ARTIFICIAL SYSTEMS

Abstract

This chapter presents the different possible routes to building an Artificial Intelligence (AI) system. On one hand, it presents the design assumptions underlying cognitive approaches to AI and, on the other, it presents the tenets of machine-oriented approaches aimed at obtaining AI systems able to exhibit intelligent behaviour without making any assumption about the biological or cognitive plausibility of the implemented mechanisms. It additionally introduces the reader to the main instances regarding the debate on the levels of analysis of computational systems (cognitively inspired or not).

Nature- vs. machine-inspired approaches to artificial systems

It is possible to draw a broad distinction between two different computational approaches for the modelling of intelligent behaviour in artificial systems. We can distinguish, indeed, between "natural/cognitive/biological" inspired systems and "machine" oriented systems. The former explicitly take inspiration (at different levels of abstraction) from natural systems, and their "heuristics", to design an equivalent artificial system able to exhibit the same intelligent behaviour by employing, to the greatest extent possible, the same mechanisms. Machine-oriented systems do not take inspiration from how nature solves problems, but rather develop algorithms and engineering solutions by focusing on the computational challenges posed by the problem itself. The latter strategy is a perfectly reasonable and useful approach to developing Artificial Intelligence (AI) algorithms by avoiding cognitive or neural inspiration as well as claims of cognitive or neural plausibility. Indeed, this is how many researchers have proceeded in the last few decades and this approach nowadays represents the mainstream research adopted in modern AI. In their influential textbook, Russell and Norvig (2002) frame this kind of approach by referring to the analogy with earlier engineering artefacts: they state that "the quest for 'artificial flight' succeeded when the Wright brothers and others stopped imitating birds and started using wind tunnels and learning about aerodynamics" (3). This excerpt suggests that taking inspiration from nature can be, somehow, a sort of drawback with respect to the strategy of pursuing a more machine-oriented approach for building useful technologies. Recent progresses in AI seem to confirm this overall hypothesis (at least for systems working on specialized and well-defined application domains). In particular, the example of the airplane and of its different flight mode with respect to birds, has become popular in AI because it points out how – from an engineering perspective – it is important to individuate the right element to investigate (i.e., the laws of the aerodynamics) in order to find different possible technical solutions. As Simon famously said, indeed, "the flight of airplanes does not much resemble the flight of birds, except in the fact that both can sometimes stay aloft" (see Simon, 1979: 203).

For the purposes of this book, this example is also relevant since it points out that the mere "functional resemblance" in terms of generated output (i.e., the ability to fly in this case) between organisms and machines is not sufficient for explaining that function through a model capable of reproducing the essential features of that organism. In other words: a similar behaviour/output can obviously be obtained through completely different processes/mechanisms. I would say that this is an important caveat to take into account when distinguishing the cognitive-oriented approach from other machine-oriented AI approaches. To better describe this difference we need to introduce the distinction, reflected in the design phase, between functional and structural artificial models.

Functionalist vs. structuralist design approaches

The distinction between functionalist and structuralist design approaches is important in the context of the debate over the explanatory role played by artificial models (and systems) with respect to their analogous natural cognitive systems that are eventually taken as source of inspiration.

Functionalism was introduced in the philosophy of mind by Hillary Putnam in his seminal article *Minds and Machines* (Putnam, 1960) as a position on the type identity of "mental states". In this context, mental states can be understood and characterized on the basis of their functional role. In particular, two tokens are assumed to belong to the same mental state if they are in the same functional relation with the other mental states and with the input/output of the system.[1]

---

1 Within the philosophical tradition, functionalism has been proposed in many different forms (for example, Jerry Fodor posed stricter requirements with respect to the functionalist analysis of the mind proposed by Putnam). We will not dwell here on these different proposals. An important theoretical notion of some functionalist accounts that, however, had an indirect impact

This approach had a direct influence on AI since, in this context, it led to the definition of what we can call a design approach based on the notion "*functional equivalence*" between some cognitive faculties to model and the corresponding mechanisms implemented in AI programs. Indeed, in that context, its more radical formulation postulated the sufficiency, from an epistemological perspective, of a weak equivalence (i.e., the equivalence in terms of functional organization) between cognitive processes and AI procedures. In other words, it posited that, from an explanatory point of view, the relation between "natural mind" and "artificial software" could have been based purely on a macroscopic *equivalence* of the *functional organization* of the two systems and their input-output specification. This position has been widely criticized in the literature over the last few decades. In particular, models and systems designed according to the "functionalist" perspective are not good candidates for advancing the science of cognitive AI since, as in the case of the airplane, the mechanisms and the overall design choices adopted to build such artefacts prevent them from having any kind of explanatory role with respect to their analogous systems available in nature. This is the case, for example, with recent AI technologies, including some self-proclaimed "cognitive computing" systems like IBM Watson or Alpha Go.[2] Despite the propaganda both in the media and the scientific literature, such systems, in fact, cannot be qualified as "cognitive" since they do not have any kind of explanatory role with respect to: (i) how humans organize, retrieve, and reason (on) the information stored in their minds when answering questions (in the case of IBM Watson) or (ii) how people make decisions when planning their next move in the game of *Go* (in the case of Alpha Go). In other words, such systems, just like the vast majority of current AI systems (including very popular ones, from Siri to Alexa or Cortana), are "functional" systems. They "function as" a natural system (in terms of the provided output, given the input that they process and in terms of the surface organization of their internal components) but the internal mechanisms determining that output are completely different with respect to what we do as humans. Therefore, a mere artificial imitation of cognitive capabilities does not necessarily function according to the same principles. As mentioned,

---

in the context of AI is the notion of "multiple realizability". This notion concerns the fact that the functional organization of different mental states can be "realized", e.g., implemented, in different physical systems (including, for example, the human brain or computer hardware). This notion was used to distinguish the functional level with respect to the physical one and, as a consequence, to point out that in order to analyze mental states, only the functional level is important. As we will see in the following sections, a similar argument concerning the minor importance of the "physical level" was expressed, although starting on different premises and focusing on "artificial" rather than "natural" systems, by Allen Newell in his "levels-based characterisation" of intelligent behaviour in artificial systems (please refer to the following pages for a more precise introduction to this issue).

2 IBM Watson is a question-answering system that defeated the human champions of a game known as *Jeopardy!* while Alpha Go is a system developed by Deep Mind (an innovative spin-off from Google) that defeated the human world champion of *Go*, a popular strategic game (mostly known in Asia). We will analyze these two systems in more detail in Chapter 4.

this is an important aspect to point out since, in many cases, attempts to ascribe cognitive explanations to functional systems are numerous (as described in the above-mentioned IBM and Google systems). This confusion also arises due to the improper use nowadays of expressions like "cognitive computing", which is usually intended as wide umbrella term to indicate the entire field of systems able to provide some kind of interaction with humans.[3]

Diverging from functionalism, there is another possible method to follow, from a design point of view: the structural approach. This approach claims the necessity of a stronger, constrained connection between the designed artificial systems, and their internal architecture and procedures, and the corresponding ones available in nature. According to such an approach, structurally constrained artificial models and systems can be useful both to advance the science of AI in terms of technological achievements (e.g., in tasks that are easily solvable for humans but very hard to solve for machines using non-cognitive inspired approaches, for instance in commonsense reasoning) and to play the role of "computational experiments", able to provide insights and results useful in refining or rethinking theoretical aspects concerning the target natural system used as source of inspiration (Cordeschi, 2002; Minkowski, 2013).

An immediate problem arising in this view is that it is not possible to build a completely structural and constrained artificial model, since it is not possible to reproduce a realistic artificial "*replica*" of a natural system.[4] The search for increasing structural models, in fact, produces an asymptotic regression to the microscopic physical world until it reaches the well-known Wiener paradox summarized in his sentence, "The best material model of a cat is another, or preferably the same, cat" (Rosenblueth and Wiener, 1945). In short, this "paradox" advocates for the realization of proxy-models, not replicas, of a given natural system by pointing out the difficulty of such a challenge. In a similar way, Pylyshyn asserted, about cognitive modelling (Pylyshyn, 1979: 49), that if we do not formulate any restriction about a model, we obtain the functionalism of Turing machine and, if we apply all possible restrictions, we reproduce a whole human being.

---

3 We will discuss in more detail in the following chapters why this kind of a usage of the term is incorrect.

4 And also when this investigation is possible, e.g., in the field of so-called "synthetic complete models" (available for very simple organisms), the aspect of interpreting the model is problematic. A famous example is the case of the nematode known as *Caenorhabditis elegans*: a very simple organism endowed with about 300 neurons, whose DNA and expression pattern mapping have been completely described by biologists. An early project aimed at building a detailed simulation model of this organism; it showed how, despite the completeness of much of the empirical data about this simple organism, the complexity of genetic and cellular interactions made a full understanding and testing of biological hypotheses extremely problematic (Kitano, Hamahashi, and Luke, 1998: 142). Based on this example, it should not be surprising that the outcome of similar projects repeated on a larger scale, like the recent Human Brain Project (aimed at providing a "whole brain computational simulation" by 2023), face the very same difficulties and represent, nowadays, an example of myopic research investment and scientific failure.

Thus, the key point here is the research of the right level of description and of the corresponding enforcement of constraints to this level to carry out human-like computation. In this view, the only way to make progress is through developing plausible structural models of our cognition, based on a more constrained equivalence between AI procedures and their corresponding cognitive processes.

A suitable solution for this state of affairs consists of considering the functionalism/structuralism dichotomy as extremes of a continuum. Between the explanatory lack of usefulness of pure functional artificial models (which, nonetheless, can achieve impressive performances in specific tasks, as shown by systems like Watson and Alpha Go) and the unfeasible realizability of pure structural models, it is possible to individuate – in between – a plethora of plausible artificial proxy-models with different degrees of explanatory power with respect to the natural systems taken as sources of inspiration.

Levels of analysis of computational systems

A further important and influential conceptual tool that is useful to introduce for the analysis of different types of artificial systems (including cognitive ones) is represented by some notorious proposals about the levels of organization through which to observe the behaviour of such systems. In this respect, different systematizations have been proposed. The first and most influential one was made by David Marr (Marr, 1977, 1982). According to Marr, the computational account of a cognitive phenomenon can be formulated at three different levels: the level of the *computational theory* (also called *level 1*), the level of *algorithms and representations* (*level 2*), and the *implementation level* (*level 3*) (Marr, 1982, Chapter 1). The level of the computational theory is the most abstract; it concerns the specification of the task associated with a given cognitive phenomenon. At this level, cognitive tasks are characterized only in terms of their input data, the results they produce, and the overall aim (the "goal") of the computation, without any reference to the specific processes and cognitive mechanisms involved. In other words, at the level of the computational theory, a cognitive task is accounted in terms of a purely functional correspondence (mapping) between inputs and outputs. The algorithmic and implementation level concerns, to different degrees of abstraction, the realization of the task described at the level of the computational theory. The aim of the algorithmic level is to specify "how" a certain task is performed: it deals with the particular procedures that are carried out and with the representation structures on which such procedures operate. The implementation level is concerned with the features of the physical device (e.g., the structures of the nervous system or of a particular artificial neural network architecture) that implement the representations and the procedures singled out at the algorithmic level. The relation that exists between a theory expressed at the computational level and the underlying algorithmic level can be regarded as the relation between a function (in a mathematical sense) that is computable and a specific algorithm for calculating its values. The aim of a computational theory is to single out a function that models the cognitive phenomenon to be studied. Within the framework of a computational approach, such a function must be effectively computable. However, at the level of the computational theory, no assumption is made about the nature of the algorithms and their implementation.

It is worth noting that Marr's levels are not specifically concerned with *cognitive* systems; rather, they pertain to the analysis of a *computational* system whatsoever. They can be applied to any system that can be studied in computational terms. Let us consider Marr's example of a machine computing arithmetic addition; Marr illustrates his tripartite analysis resorting to the example of a device whose functioning is well understood: a cash register. At the *computational* level, the functioning of the register can be accounted for in terms of arithmetic and, in particular, the theory of addition; at this level are relevant the computed function (addition) and abstract properties of it, such as commutativity or associativity (Marr, 1982: 23). The level of *representation and algorithm* specify the form of the representations and the processes elaborating them: "We might choose Arabic numerals for the representations, and for the algorithm we could follow the usual rules about adding the least significant digits first and 'carrying' if the sum exceeds 9" (*ibid.*). Finally, the level of implementation has to do with how such representations and processes are physically realized; for example, the digits could be represented as positions on a metal wheel or, alternatively, as binary numbers coded by the electrical states of digital circuitry.

Marr's distinctions are clear, theoretically well-grounded, and necessary in the context of our discourse because such dimension of analysis can be naturally mapped into the functional/structural dichotomy by extending the understanding of different types of artificial systems (whether they are cognitively inspired or not). However, in the field of cognitive science, Marr's levels have been sometimes misinterpreted and confused with other distinctions and with other "levels".

Indeed, the first confusion that has sometimes been made between Marr's levels is with the three levels proposed by Zenon Pylyshyn in his book *Cognition and Computation* (1984). In particular, Pylyshyn claims that "explaining cognitive behavior requires that we advert to three distinct levels of a system" (xviii); he terms them the *semantic*, *syntactic* (or symbolic), and *physical* (or neurophysiological) levels.

According to Pylyshyn,

> Organisms and artifacts that need to be described at the semantic level, i.e., by attributing to them goals, beliefs and desires, are those whose representations are physically instantiated, in the brain or in a hardware, as codes, i.e., as symbol structures capable of causing behavior.
>
> *(Cordeschi, 2002)*

From Pylyshyn's point of view, systems of this kind include human minds and software. The semantic level, according to Pylyshyn (1989), "explains why people, or appropriately programmed computers, do certain things by saying what they know and what their goals are and by showing that these are connected in certain meaningful or even rational ways" (57). The semantic level, then, is the one concerned with the "semantic content" of representations. The syntactic (or symbolic) level, on the other hand, concerns the way in which such semantic content of knowledge and goals is encoded and – in the Pylyshyn's view (1989: 57) – it is assumed to be encoded by symbols such as the ones assumed in the Physical Symbol Systems Hypothesis (PSSH). Finally, the physical level concerns the implementation details of the symbolic level in both brains and machines. Pylyshn also identifies three kinds of explanations corresponding to each of his levels, namely, intentional, functional, and biological explanations.

In spite of some superficial similarities, however, Marr and Pylyshyn's proposals are situated at "different levels". In the first place, there is no reason to assume that the level of computational theory has something to do with semantic content or with "intentional" explanations.[5] The highest level of Marr's hierarchy, in fact, can be characterized in terms of the well-understood mathematical concept of function, without any need to involve semantic or intentional notions. It must be also noted that Marr's levels do not pertain to the overall structure of the mind, nor do they constitute a general point of view on the mind as a whole. In other words, Marr's levels are local levels, which do not aspire to individuate a general structure of cognition; rather, they are aimed at explaining the functioning of specific cognitive or computational components.

Moreover, it is not granted that a mental process can always be studied in computational terms, i.e., according to the three levels of Marr's methodology. Marr (1977) explicitly admits that in some cases it is unlikely that an abstract characterization of the computed function (corresponding to the computational level) could be separated from a detailed description of the processes calculating its values (corresponding to the level of algorithms and of representations). For example, "this can happen when a problem is solved by the simultaneous action of a considerable number of processes, *whose interaction is its own simplest description*" (Marr, 1977).

Furthermore, it is important to stress that, in the field of the study of the mind, there is no reason to exclude that Marr's approach can be applied to both "macroscopic" (e.g., phenomena concerning natural language processing, planning, or reasoning) and "microscopic" cognitive phenomena (for example, at the level of the behaviour of single neurons). What is crucial is that they are suitable for a computational analysis.

Finally, as mentioned, Marr's levels are *local* levels. As the philosopher José Luis Bermudez correctly observes: "Marr's account ... would still fall a long

---

5 Intentional explanations can be described as explanations in which the behaviour of a system is characterized by attributing to it some "intentionality" to perform a certain task (given its knowledge about the world). As we will see, this aspect represents a crucial part of Dennet's "intentional stance" proposal.

way short of providing a picture of the mind as a whole" (Bermudez, 2005: 27) and "Marr's analysis ... is not itself pitched at the right sort of level to provide a model of how we might understand the general idea of a hierarchy of explanation applied to the mind as a whole" (*ibid.*). From the viewpoint of Bermudez, this is a *limitation* of Marr's proposal. In this respect, my evaluation is antithetical: the interest of Marr's levels lies exactly in the fact that they do not offer a questionable and premature picture of the general structure of the mind; rather, they provide a solid methodological tool for the local analysis of many cognitive phenomena. It is exactly these kinds of conceptual tools that are needed in the fields of cognitive AI and computational cognitive science.

Pylyshyn's levels of analysis are better associated with, and inspired by, another well-known "levels-based" characterization of the behaviour and analysis of artificial systems: the Knowledge, Symbol and Physical levels proposed by Allen Newell (1982). In particular, Newell posited that such a hierarchy of levels characterizes the PSSH architecture of an intelligent system. In his own words (Newell, 1982: 98): "The system at the knowledge level is the agent. The components at the knowledge level are goals, actions, and bodies. Thus, an agent is composed of a set of actions, a set of goals and a body". The medium at the knowledge level is knowledge. Thus, the agent processes its knowledge to determine the actions to take. Finally, the behaviour law is the principle of rationality: actions are selected to attain the agent's goals. According to Newell,

> To treat a system at the knowledge level is to treat it as having some knowledge and some goals, and believing it will do whatever is within its power to attain its goals, in so far as its knowledge indicates.
>
> *(Newell, 1982)*

Newell sees the knowledge level, and the "knowledge level analysis" that an AI designer has to do in his building efforts, as a central construct for understanding intelligent systems. This level needs to be used in conceit with lower-level descriptions: the Symbol Level that, as the reader can probably guess, concerns the actual representational format (the symbols) and the information-processing mechanisms used by the system in order to reach its goal (given the knowledge that it possesses), and, finally, the physical level concerning the actual physical implementation of such symbolic structures.[6] The knowledge, symbol, and physical levels of Newell clearly correspond to the *semantic, syntactic,* and *physical* (or neurophysiological) levels of Pylyshyn. As in that case, however, it is not possible to equate Newell's knowledge level with Marr's computational level since they are different dimensions through which to analyze (and also design) intelligent behaviour. Similarly, a mapping between the Marr's representation

---

6 Following the PSSH (introduced in Chapter 1), the physical or "hardware" level is considered less important by Newell in order to understand the emergence of intelligent behaviours in artificial systems.

and algorithmic level and the syntactic (à la Pylyshyn) or the symbolic (à la Newell) levels is misleading, since Marr's analytical tool does not make any assumption about the nature of the representations and algorithms, while Pylyshyn and Newell are explicitly rooted in the PSSH. Finally, a similar discourse holds also for the physical or implementation levels in all three different accounts. More specifically, this level seems to be the most "compliant" one between all the proposals, but this is only due to the fact that it is highly underspecified in both Pylyshyn's and Newell's theoretical constructs.

Interestingly enough, however, both Pylyshyn's and Newell's levels of analysis can be (partially) related to another important piece of cognitive literature about the strategies used for explaining and understanding the behaviour of an intelligent system (be it natural or artificial): the different "stances", i.e., explanatory attitudes, individuated by Daniel Dennett.

Dennett, in particular, individuates the so-called *physical, design,* and *intentional stance* for explaining the behaviour of a system (Dennett, 1976, 1988). An example to explain these different strategies is the following: if we consider chemists or physicists in their laboratories, studying certain kinds of molecules, we can imagine that they try to explain (or predict) the molecules' behaviour through the laws of physics. This is what Dennett calls the "physical stance". There are cases, however, in which such laws are an inadequate (or not the most efficient) way to predict the behaviour of a system. For example, when we ride a bike, we can fairly predict that the speed will decrease if we push on the brakes, since the bike itself is designed this way. To make this kind of prediction, however, we do not need to know the precise physical mechanisms behind all atoms and molecules in the braking system of the bike, but it is sufficient to rely on our experience and knowledge of how the bike is designed. Dennett describes this as the "design stance". The third strategy proposed by him, the intentional stance, corresponds to the attitude – assumed by a human observer – of attributing "intentionality" to a given system, whether biological or artificial, as an option for the observer to understand and explain its behaviour. As Dennett states:

> There is another stance or strategy that one can adopt: the intentional stance. Here is how it works: first you decide to treat the object whose behavior is to be predicted as a rational agent; then you figure out what beliefs that agent ought to have, given its place in the world and its purpose. Then you figure out what desires it ought to have, on the same considerations, and finally you predict that this rational agent will act to further its goals in the light of its beliefs. A little practical reasoning from the chosen set of beliefs and desires will in many – but not in all – instances yield a decision about what the agent ought to do; that is what you predict the agent will do.
>
> *(Dennett, 1988: 17)*

In Dennett's view, "there is no difference between attributing intentionality to a car, a thermostat or a program: the intentionality of any artifact is always 'derived' from that, 'intrinsic' or 'original,' of its designer" (Cordeschi, 2002: 261). In addition, according to him, a system does not necessarily have to have representations in order to be "intentionally" described in terms of beliefs, purposes, and desires; it is sufficient for it to behave as if it were a rational agent. This assumption was critiqued by *computationalists*[7] à la Fodor (Fodor, 1986) and, as should be evident, also contrasts with the underlying symbolic-grounded assumptions made by both Newell and Pylyshyn.

A point of contact, however, can be for sure traced between the intentional stance and both the "semantic level" proposed by Pylyshyn – explicitly asking for an "intentional" explanation,[8] and therefore an "intentional stance" assumed by the observer with respect to the observed system – and Newell's "knowledge level". As Newell himself admits (Newell, 1988: 2):

> At about the time that Brainstorms was published, I discussed a construct that I called the knowledge level (Newell, 1982). I did this in the context of a AAAI presidential address, as pan of my general view that computer science and AI, by their practice, have homed in on essentially correct notions of several central concepts in cognitive science, in particular symbols (Newell & Simon, 1976; Newell, 1980) and knowledge (Newell, 1982; Newell, 1986), but perhaps others as well, such as the architecture. Before I finished preparing that address, I found and read Brainstorms. It was instantly clear that the knowledge level and the intentional stance are fundamentally the same, and I indicated as much in the talk. Dan's assessment seems to agree (Dennett, 1986). Thus, there is no question about the basic relationship between the two they are formulations of the same solution.

Despite this conceptual alignment at the surface level, however, it is Newell himself who pointed out some differences between these two theoretical formulations (Newell, 1988). Among those individuated by him (for details I recommend reading Newell, 1988), the most relevant ones, for the purposes of this book, are: the "stance versus system" view and the "technical development" argument. In regards to the former, Newell argues that Dennett's theory refers to "stances" – and therefore take an "observer" point of view – while his theory refers to "systems". Newell's levels, in fact, are intrinsically system-oriented: i.e.,

---

7 Computationalism is a philosophical view that claims that the mental processes of the mind are computations or, more precisely, that "the theoretical constructs of a theory of the mind are both the computational processes that are supposed to occur in the mind and the data structures ('representations') that such processes manipulate" (Cordeschi and Frixione, 2007). Some of its main assumptions are borrowed from informational processing psychology but is should not be confused, as it has been unfortunately done, with both Newell and Simon's PSSH and Fodor's theory of Language of Thought (see Cordeschi and Frixione, 2007, for a detailed account of these aspects).

8 We anticipate here that intentional explanations can be seen as a type of so-called "teleological explanations", which will be introduced in Chapter 3.

they describe a hierarchy of a general system architecture. These are obviously different aspects of situations where analysts, who take stances, describe parts of reality as systems of various types. This aspect is related also to the second point raised by Newell: the technical development issue. He correctly points out that the knowledge level view has had a concrete technical impact in the field of AI, while Dennett's intentional stance has had no technical development and impact at all within the AI community, in both the design and development of AI systems (I assume that I will not be too far from the truth if I say that the youngest AI researchers do not know at all what the "intentional stance" is). Nonetheless, Dennett's contribution (which, by the way, was the first to come from a historical perspective) has provided, as we will see better in the Chapter 3, important insights for aspects concerning the explanatory role ascribed to both cognitive and non-cognitive artificial systems.

The space of cognitive systems

In his 2014 book *Artificial Cognitive Systems*, the cognitive roboticist David Vernon proposed a 2D space for the classification of different types of cognitive artificial systems. Its original 2D space considered on the x-axis the level of natural (i.e., biological or cognitive) inspiration assumed for the design of an artificial system (with the extremes of "machine-oriented" and "natural inspiration") and, on the y-axis, the level of abstraction of the modelling tools adopted for modelling the behaviour of an artificial system (with the extremes being "high" and "low"). In light of the arguments presented so far, that original schema has been "enriched" by considering and making explicit two other elements that were left implicit in Vernon's analysis: the kind of design approach considered (functionalist vs. structuralist) and the type of modelling approach considered (symbolic vs. emergentist).

This *"Enriched 2D Space of Cognitive Systems"* is depicted in Figure 2.1.

The proposed enrichment serves the scope of showing that it is possible to have functionalist or structural systems using both the symbolic and emergentist

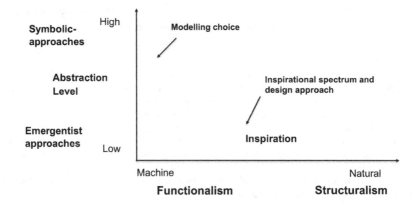

FIGURE 2.1 Enriched 2D space of cognitive systems.

approaches. Therefore, selecting the modelling paradigms to adopt in the realization phase involves design choices at the representational/algorithmic level (*level 2* in Marr's terms) but is, in principle, not relevant for the explanatory ability of the artificial systems with respect to their analogous nature.[9] It is important to point this aspect out because, as indicated in the previous chapter, the last few decades of research in the fields of Cognitive Science and AI have shown empirically that both emergentist and symbolic approaches are useful in modelling different aspects of cognitive capacities in artificial systems. Indeed, low-level (e.g., perceptual, motor, etc.) capabilities of artificial systems are usually better modelled by using emergent approaches, while high-level (e.g., reasoning) cognitive capacities are better modelled by adopting a symbolic approach. Therefore, the cognitive design perspective, and the corresponding explanatory power of the behaviour of artificial systems, is in principle agnostic with respect to the classes of formalisms applied to model a given phenomenon; it can be applied to both the symbolic and emergentist research agendas.

A natural consequence of this state of affairs is that it becomes possible to realize "structurally plausible" cognitive artificial systems (or artificial models of cognition) by adopting modelling frameworks focusing on different levels of abstraction. This aspect is important because there is nowadays an implicit *vulgata* in considering as "structurally valid models" only those adopting some of the emergentist modelling approaches. However, based on what we have discussed so far, it should be clear by now that this assumption is methodologically wrong. As we will see, in fact, adopting an emergentist modelling framework (e.g. let's say a connectionist one) does not in itself imply satisfying the requirement of *biological plausibility*. We can have models based on the functional organization of neural nets with suitable learning algorithms without such models being biologically plausible or interesting as explanatory tools. As pointed out by Cordeschi (2002: 255):

> The very question of "model indeterminacy", raised by the functional equivalence by the symbolic approaches to the way in which our brain processes information, could be similarly raised by the functional equivalence at the neural net level, if the appropriate constraints are not identified.

For the very same argument, it is not possible to exclude *a priori* symbolic systems from the list of potentially plausible models of cognition. In fact, even if nowadays there is no neuroscientific evidence of the existence of "symbols" in our brain à la PSSH, it is true that from a functional point of view that our biological neural architecture is able to organize in a hierarchical and efficient way its neural representations such that the more abstract neural layers of this hierarchy behave like a symbol (and therefore can account for all types of manipulations and combinations executed and described by symbolic systems). In addition, such symbol-like

---

9 As we will see, the "explanatory power" depends on the types of structural constraints considered during the modelling phase.

structures can still be combined among them in a cognitively compliant way (i.e., according to cognitively plausible information processing mechanisms), thus contributing to the realization of structurally plausible artificial models. We will examine this aspect in the following section with some examples.

Functional and structural neural systems

As mentioned in the previous chapter, among the different formalisms of bio-inspired computing aimed at creating intelligent systems by imitating the brain, neural networks are one of the most adopted modelling paradigms. The first models of artificial neural networks, however, proved to be too simplistic and not similar to the brain (Forbes, 2004) (i.e., they were simplistic functional models).

Nevertheless, they inspired statisticians and computer scientists to develop very successful non-linear statistical models and learning algorithms that comprise an important part of *machine learning*[10] techniques today. The recent resurgence of interest in neural networks, more commonly referred to as "deep neural networks" or "deep learning models",[11] share the same representational commitments and often even the same learning algorithms as the earlier PDP models. For example, most neural networks use some form of gradient-based learning rules (e.g., backpropagation). It has long been argued, however, that backpropagation is not biologically plausible. For example, as Francis Crick (1989) famously pointed out, backpropagation requires that information be transmitted backwards along the axon. However, this phenomenon has never been observed in natural neural architectures and, therefore, cannot be considered a realistic mechanism. This evidence has not prevented backpropagation from being put to good use in connectionist models of cognition (e.g., in the computational models of cognition proposed by Rumelhart, McClelland, and the PDP Research Group, 1986) or in building deep neural networks for AI systems. In all these cases, in fact – and in particular the case of the connectionist models of cognition – the realism of such models is based on the presence of additional constraints (if any) that come directly from the anatomo-physiological knowledge of real, biological, neural networks (a classic example confirming this fact is represented by the work of Churchland and Sejnowski [1992], which showed how

---

10 Machine learning represents a subfield of AI focusing on the development of automatic techniques for allowing machines to learn and abstract regularities from raw data. Deep learning techniques represent a subset of machine learning.

11 Deep neural networks, used in deep learning technologies, present many intermediate layers between the input and output units (usually hundreds of layers), thus creating a "deep" hierarchy of connections. The key idea of deep learning is that at each layer it is possible to learn features of increasing abstraction with respect to the previous layer (Goodfellow et al., 2016). For example, in a vision setting, the lowest level learns lines and edges, the next layer may learn corners and curves, the next layer may learn simple shapes, and so on up the hierarchy. Upper levels are supposed to then learn complex categories (cars, people, dogs) or even specific instances (your dog, your cat, etc.).

different neurophysiological hypotheses about the vestibule-eye circuit could have been modelled by different neural net models providing different results to evaluate). Such constraints, once identified and put in place, provide what we are prepared to consider plausible models for the sake of explanation.[12] We need to keep in mind, however, that every model, even the most realistic one, is so at a certain level of abstraction and simplification of reality. Therefore, in the class of "biologically inspired" modelling methods and techniques also, it is possible to individuate a continuum between functional and structural artificial nets.

As pointed out by Shayani (2013), the field of artificial neural networks (apart from the boom in deep learning technologies) is attracting new attention thanks to the development of different types of novel, bio-inspired neural models. The author, for example, points out how spiking neural neuron models and Hierarchical Temporal Memory (HTM) represent two of the most interesting novelties of the last few years in this respect. Spiking neural networks – characterized by the fact that the activation of individual neurons resembles the one in biological neurons, which communicate via discrete spikes of voltage – have shown some advantages in power consumption (since spikes can be routed like data packets) and have been proven to result in computationally more powerful networks than classical ANNs. In addition, spiking recurrent neural nets, a variant of classical spiking neural models, have been proven to be more robust to noise and more efficient than classical ANNs in processing spatiotemporal data. HTM networks, on the other hand, have received interest due to their biological inspiration, taken from the characteristics of the mammalian brain. The main idea of these networks, introduced by Hawkins, is that there is a single common structure and algorithm controlling many different functions of the neocortex (from vision to language and motor planning, etc.). Among the main biological assumptions of HTM there is the importance of the temporal persistence of the causes (objects) in such networks (Hawkins and Blakeslee, 2005), as well as the use of sparse coding and Recurrent Neural Nets for spatiotemporal pattern recognition.

An additional effort towards establishing the biological plausibility of ANNs is pursued with the so-called "evo-devo networks", incorporating evolutionary computing algorithms[13] that allow the network to adapt to a changing environment

12 Michael A. Arbib has been one of the most influential figures in brain-inspired neural network models. A classic reference in the field is the *Handbook of Brain Theories and Neural Networks* (Arbib, 2002). In a more recent memoir, Arbib illustrates the role of the classic contributions of cybernetics in building constrained models in the context of computational neuroscience (Arbib, 2018).

13 Evolutionary Computation is a subfield of AI that adopts iterative heuristic techniques and algorithms inspired by the evolutionary processes of "growth" and "selection". Swarm intelligence, genetic programming, evolutionary programming, evolutionary strategies, and evolutionary algorithms represent different subsets of techniques, partially intersecting, belonging to the field of evolutionary computation. In particular, one of the most well-known algorithms adopted in this field are Genetic Algorithms (GA) (Holland, 1975). Evolutionary algorithms, in general, are known to be good meta-heuristic optimization and search techniques, where there is little to no knowledge about the search space.

and guarantee more robustness and optimization capabilities for specific problems. In particular, the inclusion of evolutionary heuristics in bio-plausible neurodevelopment-constrained networks leverages the emergence of features such as fault-tolerance, self-organization, regeneration, and self-repair, and meanwhile also improves the evolvability and scalability of the system (Shayani, 2013: 1). A side effect of including all such constraints in neural models, however, is that it makes it necessary to have very powerful hardware platforms able to execute the computation on such networks. This problem is nowadays well-handled thanks to the development of new technologies like Field Programmable Gate Arrays (FPGAs) or via the exploitation of GPUs (Graphical Processing Units) that are able to alleviate the issue. Mentioning all this plethora of neural network solutions is important for the purposes of the book, since these architectures – and many others that are available on the "connectionist market" – have, as has been described, different degrees of plausibility. Therefore, the functional/structural continuum applies to this class of modelling techniques as well. In the next section, we will show how the same dichotomy also applies to the class of symbolic formalisms.

Functional and structural symbolic systems

Symbolic approaches, as mentioned in Chapter 1, are a family of different approaches relying on a plethora of problem-solving strategies and representational assumptions ranging from classical logic to probabilistic, fuzzy, default, and different non-monotonic extensions. As for connectionist modelling frameworks, the adoption of such a family of approaches to model cognitive faculties in artificial systems can be also seen through the functional/structural continuum. As mentioned, different types of novel and more flexible symbolic formalisms have been proposed over the last few decades, in order to overcome a foundational problem of symbolic approaches relying on classical logic: dealing with commonsense reasoning.

In a commonsense situation, in fact, agents do not have access to complete information about the environment and about its changes. This can lead to situations in which, when new knowledge is acquired, the previously drawn conclusions need to be withdrawn and revised (technically these are called *defeasible* or *non-monotonic inferences*). This process cannot happen in classical or monotonic logic where, once a conclusion is deductively derived from certain premises, it continues to hold even if new premises (i.e., new knowledge) is added. A classic example of a simple non-monotonic inference is the following: if x is a bird (premise), then x can fly (conclusion). But if one comes to know that x is a penguin (a further premise), one has to reconsider the conclusion previously accepted. These kinds of inferences are usually tackled in non-monotonic approaches by resorting to so-called "*defaults*" (i.e., established generalizations about certain states of affairs presumed to be true until proven otherwise, introduced in Reiter, 1980). For example: one can typically assume that the "default" number of legs of a dog is four, but a dog with three legs would still belong to the "dog frame" (to use Minsky's terminology).

Within the class of non-monotonic approaches to reasoning, John McCarthy[14] proposed the idea of a logical system with "circumscription" (McCarthy, 1980). His idea was to circumscribe as "anomalous" potential exceptions to a typical situation, like the one stated by the sentence: "If x is a bird, then x can fly". In this case, the property of "non-flying" is anomalous with respect to "being a bird" and, thus, such an anomalous property is circumscribed. In other words, this property is assumed to have the smallest possible extension with respect to the information at one's disposal. The sentence in the example, therefore, is reformulated as follows: "If x is a bird, and x is not an anomalous bird, then x can fly". The investigation of such problems provided the background for a whole series of research projects – which were then called "logicist" – on the use of logic as a medium for representing the commonsense knowledge that is at the core of the agent's model of the world. However,

> these investigations rarely provided suggestions for actual implementation or, in general, for the solution of heuristic reasoning problems. Thus one often witnessed a proliferation of investigations into various forms of circumscription and non-monotonic rules, which also led to some defections.
>
> *(Cordeschi, 2002: 202)*

Similarly, other important contributions came from the development of other types of logic: fuzzy, modal, temporal, etc. Within these approaches, the fuzzy logic introduced by Lofti Zadeh (1988), rejecting the idea of having a rigid characterization of conceptual structures, was a particularly interesting way to deal with the problem of commonsense reasoning. Fuzzy logic methods, however, despite initial expectations and despite having been used successfully in many real-world applications, have not proven to be an adequate foundation for many commonsense reasoning tasks. As evidence of this state of affairs, it is worth noting that almost all successful fuzzy logic applications are applied embedded controllers, while most theoretical papers on fuzzy methods dealing with knowledge representation and reasoning have not provided the expected results.

All these different types of symbolic approaches can be seen as approaches collocating in different positions in the functional vs. structural continuum.

---

14 John McCarthy was the first researcher to propose the use of logic to endow machines with commonsense reasoning capabilities. His first proposal was for a hypothetical logical system that he named the "Advice Taker" (McCarthy, 1960). The Advice Taker was conceived as a general or multi-purpose problem-solving system, formulating plans and drawing inferences based on a sufficiently extensive body of knowledge, while also making use of "advice" provided by its programmer. The Advice Taker, just like the GPS, aimed at being a "general" system. The main, crucial difference among the two systems was that, in the McCarthy proposal, the logic – and, in particular, the first order logic – was assumed to be the only language to represent knowledge and heuristics to be applied on such knowledge. In GPS, on the other hand, logical representations were only one of the possible "symbolic" accounts handled by the heuristic program.

Probabilistic, fuzzy, and non-monotonic reasoning formalisms, in fact, augment the functional similarity between human and artificial capabilities (since they are more flexible than classical logics) but there is no evidence that they are a structurally adequate model of human reasoning and understanding (in many cases there is direct or indirect evidence to the contrary).

What is important to note, however, is that even in the most classical formulations, symbolic systems – even if structurally inadequate from a neuroscientific point of view – can be a useful means to model a computational enquiry able to discover a structural hypothesis of our reasoning mechanisms.

Again, another classical example (reported also in Minkowski, 2013) can be taken from the past. Let us consider the classical context of well-known cryptarithmetic problems having the form: DONALD + GERALD = ROBERT (Newell and Simon, 1972). In this case, ten distinct digits must be substituted for the ten distinct letters in such a way that the resulting expression is a correct arithmetic sum (526485 + 197485 = 723970). As in the usual proposal of the problem, the hint is given that D = 5. Almost all subjects who solve the problem find the values for the individual letters in a particular sequence: T = 0, E = 9, R = 7, A = 4, and so on. The reason is that only if this order is followed can each value be found definitely without considering possible combinations with the values of the other letters. With this order, in fact, the solver does not have to remember what alternative values he has assigned to other variables, nor would he have to back up if he finds that a combination of assignments has led to a contradiction. In other words, the search behaviour of the information-processing system derives directly from the system's small short-term memory capacity. In addition, the empirical fact that solvers do make the assignments in roughly this same order provides an important piece of evidence (others can be obtained by analyzing thinking-aloud protocols and eye movements) that the human information-processing system operates, in certain situations, as a serial system with limited short-term memory. In this case, in fact, the performance of the information processing system matches the verbal protocol. Furthermore, when the comparison was done with eye movements, the match between the system behaviour and human data is also higher than the agreement with verbal protocol (since verbal protocols do not mirror thinking exactly). In other words, the symbolic model usually adopted for this problem describes heuristic as "transformation in a problem space". Such model does not consider neurological constraints and, as such, cannot be considered a structural model of brain processing. The system, in fact, is compared with human solvers in a functional way. However, it makes assumptions about the algorithmic level of the problem from an information processing perspective (e.g., the constraints about the space and memory limits, the sequential processing, and so on) and, as shown, can be useful in providing structural information about the processing modes and mechanisms of the overall system. As a consequence, as in the neural models, it has its own place within the cognitive AI and cognitive modelling research agendas.

3

PRINCIPLES OF THE COGNITIVE DESIGN APPROACH

Abstract

This chapter introduces the classical notions of rationality developed in the field of cognitive modelling and presents different types of explanatory accounts available in the literature. Finally, it presents the "Minimal Cognitive Grid", a pragmatic methodological tool proposed to rank the different degrees of structural accuracy of artificial systems in order project and predict their explanatory power.

Classical, bounded, and bounded-rational models of cognition

A complementary distinction to consider, with respect to the "functional" vs. "structural" dichotomy seen in the previous chapter, is the difference between diverse types of models that can be assumed as a starting point for the design of intelligent, "rational" agents.

In particular, the main distinction lies between models of classical rationality (CR), bounded models (RM), and bounded-rational models (BRM). All of them make different design assumptions about how to build artificial minds and are based on different theories that try to explain and predict intelligent behaviour by assuming the cognitive mechanisms driving it. The first type, i.e., CR ones, were developed in the so-called classical theory of decision making, which was dominant at the beginning of the previous century, according to which humans were seen as perfectly rational agents, able to make optimal decisions via a maximization of their expected utility in any give situation.[1] Such a view, known

---

1 The theory of expected utility was originally hypothesized by Bernoulli in his book *Specimen theoriae novae de mensura sortis*, published in 1738 and translated and printed in *Econometrica* in 1954 with the title "Exposition of a New Theory on the Measurement of Risk". Here, he

in literature as "classical rationality", poses several problems from a modelling perspective, since building an "unconstrained" rational agent is a computationally intractable problem, that is, there exists no general tractable procedure (i.e., whose complexity is, at most, polynomial-time) that, for any given situation, selects an action with maximum expected utility (Bossaerts, Yadav, and Murawski, 2019).[2]

The first scholar who pointed out how CR models were cognitively implausible and, therefore, had no explanatory role with respect to the choices made by humans operating in an uncertain environment and with incomplete information, was Herbert Simon (Simon, 1947, 1955). In particular, by introducing the notion of "bounded rationality", he showed that human behaviour and decision making is "bounded" and limited by a number of both environmental and cognitive constraints and has nothing to do with optimal decision making. Through such a notion, Simon pointed out the cognitive limits (e.g., of memory storage, processing, reasoning, etc.) that human decision makers have to face when they make decisions in real life situations. According to Simon, such limits lead humans to adopt "bounded", i.e., non-optimal (but "*satisficing*" – a term he coined), solution strategies when they have to make decisions. The evidence of our "bounded rationality", reinforced years later by the work of the psychologists Amos Tversky and Daniel Kahneman on the different types of biases affecting our decision making, has led to the development of different types of theories aiming at dealing with the problem of modelling rational behaviour in bounded artificial agents. In particular, the underlying hypothesis assumed in the cognitive modelling and cognitive AI communities has been that, in order to let the intelligent behaviour emerge in nature-inspired artificial systems, it is necessary

---

proposed a solution to the so-called "St. Petersburg paradox", a well-known paradox in the context of decision theory, based on the notion of "utility" (a different dimension with respect to the classical ones concerning, for example, "monetary gain"). This notion was later introduced and systematized in Game Theory by Von Neumann and Morgenstern (see Morgenstern and Von Neumann, 1953). In general, in the latter setting, preference relations are usually modelled by means of utility functions defined on a set of alternatives with values in a suitable set of numbers (usually, real numbers). The decision model of this theory assumes an optimal (i.e., unbounded) decision maker able to calculate and choose, in each phase of problem solving, the move that maximizes the utility function. As reported in Gigerenzer (2019), "This basic theory has been modified in many ways, such as in prospect theory, and the learning of probabilities has been modeled by Bayes' rule". However, despite their widespread use, theories of expected utility maximization and unconstrained "optimality" have been criticized as being computationally intractable, assuming perfect knowledge, and lacking empirical evidence about the existence of stable utility functions over time (e.g., Friedman et al., 2014). As pointed out by Gigerenzer, Bayesian models of cognition – which are nowadays gaining attention since they provide predictive accounts (at Marr's computational level) of many cognitive phenomena – should be considered "optimality-seeking" models. As such, they encounter the problems mentioned above.

2 On the importance of including computational complexity considerations within a computational theory of cognitive competences see Frixione (2001).

to embed at least part of such constraints in the design and implementation of such systems.

A first proposal was made by the Carnegie Mellon psychologist John Anderson and his Rational Analysis (RA) approach (Anderson, 1990). Anderson proposed thinking of cognition as a set of "optimal solutions" to the adaptation problems an agent has to face. From this perspective, in order to analyze and explain cognitive behaviour at the computational level, one should start by hypothesizing a behavioural function that is optimal, given the agent's goals and environment. To use Anderson's own words:

> We can understand a lot about human cognition without considering in detail what is inside the human head. Rather, we can look in detail at what is outside the human head and try to determine what would be optimal behavior given the structure of the environment and the goals of the human.
>
> *(Anderson, 1990: 3)*

This approach may seem to be in conflict with the idea of bounded rationality, but the scientists championing "rational models" *à la* Anderson assume that our "bounded" rationality represents – de facto – an optimal configuration strategy from an evolutionary and ecological point of view. This means that evolutionarily optimal strategies considered "rational" under the RA theory (e.g., a sort of "global optima") may not necessarily coincide with some local optima decisions that could be made by adopting a maximization procedure via expected utility (as proposed by CR theorists). In other words, evolutionary shaped heuristics (e.g., let's say the "conjunction fallacy", see Tversky and Kahneman, 1983) considered "optimal" in Anderson's account of RA, cannot necessarily be the "best" local strategy to follow in a decision problem *à la* Linda.[3]

Based on these assumptions, Anderson has created the modelling paradigm known as "Rational Analysis" (Anderson, 1990; Chater and Oaksford, 1999),

---

3 The conjunction fallacy is a well-known "reasoning error" discovered by Tversky and Kahneman. It can be summarized with their famous "Linda example": let us suppose that Linda is a 31-year-old, single, outspoken, and bright lady. She majored in philosophy and was concerned with issues of discrimination and social justice, and also participated in anti-nuclear demonstrations. When asked to rank the probability of the statements (1) "Linda is a bank teller" and (2) "Linda is a bank teller and is active in the feminist movement", the majority of people rank (2) as more probable than (1), violating classic probability rules. Upon a more detailed analysis, this "error" – as all other "cognitive biases" – can be actually seen as a powerful evolutionary heuristic. Consider, for example, the following variant of the Linda problem. Let us suppose that a certain individual "Pluto" is described as follows: he weighs about 250 kg and is approximately 2 m tall. His body is covered with thick, dark fur; he has a large mouth with robust teeth and paws with long claws. He roars and growls. Now, given this information, we have to evaluate the plausibility of the two following alternatives: (a) Pluto is a mammal; (b) Pluto is a mammal, and he is wild and dangerous. Which is the "correct" answer? According to the dictates of the normative theory of probability, it is surely (a). But if you encounter Pluto in the wilderness, it would probably be best to run.

which derives models of human behaviour starting from structural environmental assumptions (the environment has a crucial role to play in this perspective) according to this iterative procedure consisting of six steps:

1   Specify precisely the goals of the cognitive system.
2   Develop a formal model of the environment to which the system is adapted.
3   Make minimal assumptions about computational limitations (of the system).
4   Derive the optimal behavioural function given 1–3 above.
5   Examine the empirical evidence to see whether the predictions of the behavioural function are confirmed.
6   Repeat; iteratively refine the theory.

This kind of modelling paradigm, in particular, has been explicitly adopted to develop ACT-R, one of the most important cognitive architectures currently available in both the cognitive modelling and cognitive AI communities (we will return to this system, and to other cognitive architectures, in the next chapter).

Despite the importance of the proposal made by Anderson, the RA paradigm, however, has also been severely criticized in the cognitive modelling community. For example Rich et al. (2020), have pointed out how many modellers have often ignored both steps 3 and 4 of RA approach and the constraints of "minimal assumptions" have sometimes been interpreted as "no assumptions at all" (Chater et al., 2003: 69). As an additional problem, RA – even when correctly interpreted – may yield to intractable behavioural functions since it goes too far in proposing that agents behave optimally without qualification and without considering proper computational limitations. In particular, the problem is that finding these evolutionary driven global optima (and deciding which ones to use) often "requires far more resources than are available" (Rich et al., 2020).

Resource-rationality models

The previous problematic considerations of RA models led to the development of the so-called "Resource-Rationality" (RR) paradigm (a sort of evolution of the RA paradigm), which tries to incorporate additional constraints with regard to those minimally hypothesized by RA models. Such constraints also consider, for example, which cognitive operations are actually available to a cognitive agent, as well as their time and cost demands. In some senses, the RR paradigm allows the development of "bounded optimal" models (where "optimality" refers to the evolutionary account given by Anderson) by incorporating additional cognitive constraints other than those shaped by evolution (or, using terminology introduced in the previous chapter, we could say that such a paradigm proposes the adoption of more "structural" constraints). The overall idea is that such "bounded optimal" models can then be more easily translated in computer simulations since computer scientists and AI researchers have already developed a theory of rationality that accounts for limited computational resources (Horvitz,

Cooper, and Heckerman, 1989; Russell and Subramanian, 1995). In particular, "bounded optimality" is a theory for designing optimal programs for agents with performance-limited hardware that must interact with their environments in real time. In this setting, "a program is bounded-optimal for a given architecture if it enables that architecture to perform as well as or better than any other program the architecture could execute instead" (Lieder and Griffiths, 2019).

Within the RR theory, the kind of constraints considered are described as follows by Lieder and Griffiths (2019: 15):

> Our theory assumes that the cognitive limitations inherent in the biologically feasible minds include a limited set of elementary operations (e.g., counting and memory recall are available but applying Bayes' theorem is not), limited processing speed (each operation takes a certain amount of time), and potentially other constraints, such as limited working memory. Critically, the world state is constantly changing as the mind deliberates. Thus, performing well requires the bounded optimal mind to not only generate good decisions but to do so quickly. Since each cognitive operation takes time, bounded optimality often requires computational frugality.

In other words, differing from the RA hypothesis, the guiding premise of RR is that resource limitations must be considered as *built-in features* from the start. The modelling approach for building RR models is summarized in the following five steps:

1   Start with a computational-level (i.e., functional) description of an aspect of cognition formulated as a problem and its solution.
2   Posit which class of algorithms the mind's computational architecture might use to approximately solve this problem, a cost in computational resources used by these algorithms, and the utility of more accurately approximating the correct solution.
3   Find the algorithm in this class that optimally trades off resources and approximation accuracy.
4   Evaluate the predictions of the resulting rational process model against empirical data.
5   Refine the computational-level theory (Step 1) or assumed computational architecture and its constraints (Step 2) to address significant discrepancies, derive a refined resource-rational model, and then reiterate or stop. (Lieder and Griffiths, 2019: 21)

So, the starting point is the computational level of analysis introduced by Marr (1982) that we discussed in the previous chapter. Once the function of the studied cognitive capacity has been individuated, the RR paradigm suggests postulating, in functional terms, an abstract computational architecture.

Next (Steps 2–3), the RR approach asks for an analysis of the possible types of algorithms that can optimally solve the problem identified at the computational level, thereby pushing the principles of rational analysis toward Marr's algorithmic level. Once the model is ready and implemented, its predictions are tested against empirical data. The results can be used to both refine the theory's assumptions about the computational architecture and the problem to be solved.

This refinement step can lead to a reiteration of the whole RR procedure (starting from Step 1) and can be repeated until the derived model becomes more structurally accurate.

As we saw in the previous chapter, the redefinition of a model's assumptions may include moving from an abstract computational architecture to increasingly constrained models of the mind or brain (depending on the modelling focus and paradigms used).

The (eventually increased) accuracy of the updated models is indirectly observed via the progressive alignments (if any) between the model predictions and the empirical data. Therefore, the underlying idea is that the results obtained via the implemented system are predictors of how the RR model is increasingly (or decreasingly) closer to the neuro-physical or psychological mechanisms determining human's responses.

The overall RR process terminates when either the model's predictions are accurate enough or all relevant cognitive constraints have been incorporated sensibly (Griffiths, Lieder, and Goodman, 2015).

Theories such as the RR, also called "optimization under constraints" theories, have been criticized by competing research programmes for various reasons. One raised objection, similar to the one against the RA approach, is that including constraints in the optimization problem does not make optimization feasible; instead, it makes it harder, so the problem remains intractable. As Gigerenzer, Hertwig, and Pachur (2011: xx) wrote, optimization "becomes more demanding mathematically with each constraint added". Gigerenzer, in particular, is the main proponent of an alternative theory of human decision making known as Adaptive Toolbox (AT). In this framework, heuristics have a crucial importance since they are considered the basic cognitive tools that compose the "adaptive toolbox" of intelligent living organisms (Gigerenzer, 2000; Gigerenzer, Hertwig, and Pachur, 2011). Interestingly enough, in this framework, as in the original RA accounts of Anderson, some classical decision-making errors and biases are considered powerful – yet fallible – heuristics to make decision in uncertain environments. The AT theory is then designed to avoid the intractability problems ascribed to the CR, RA, and RR accounts, since it assumes that intelligent agents adopt very simple decision strategies that are successful only because they are contextually appropriate. Of course, the questions about "how 'ecologically rational' agents are" and "how well any particular heuristic does in any particular environment" are empirical ones and can only be answered via experiments (Goldstein and Gigerenzer, 2002).

It is important to point out, however, that the AT's and RR's methodologies are antithetical since the latter requires considering strong rationality assumptions (and constraints) to derive empirical hypotheses; AT, on the other hand, asks about rationality only once the descriptive facts have been laid out. In addition, the AT theory does not consider relevant the appeals to optimization, since it argues that cognition is not optimized and does not necessarily perform optimally in any sense (Rich et al., 2020).

As with RR and RA, however, a critique of the AT theory is that determining in any given case which heuristic to select and apply from our cognitive repertoire is perhaps, again, a very difficult decision problem (Wallin and Gärdenfors, 2000) that, from a computational point of view, can lead, again, to intractable solutions. In order to cope with this, RR theorists have proposed including the AT framework in their theoretical apparatus by suggesting that potentially intractable resource-rational decision problems could have been approximately solved by resorting to some of the heuristics proposed by the AT theory (thus combining the two approaches). This has required them postulating an additional (resource-rational) process that yields such heuristics (Lieder and Griffiths, 2019) consisting of a simple meta-heuristic for selecting the AT heuristics. The claim is that the selected heuristics, usually shaped by evolution and simply activated on requests, generally are those leading to decent, "good enough" decisions.

This solution seems to combine the many different modelling and analytics proposals: RA, RR, and AT. It is important, however, to point out that the role of heuristics – and of the other mentioned components – was already emphasized by Simon. As early as 1955, indeed, he seemed to propose a way to put together the most relevant pieces of the theories that would be developed in the following years. Simon (1955), in fact, argued that "rational decision strategies" (i.e., the "*satisficing*" ones, in his terminology) are those adapted to both the structure of the environment (a crucial element of the RA) and to the mind's cognitive limitations (the main focus of RR paradigms). He additionally suggested that the pressure for adaptation makes it rational to use heuristics (the key point of the AT paradigm) that select the first option that is "good enough" instead of trying to find the ideal option. In other words, Simon's ideas inspired each of the three main framework developed in the cognitive modelling community and their integration in search of feasible structural models of cognition.

Kinds of explanations

The assessment of the explanatory role of computational artefacts is a debated problem in the field of computational Cognitive Science.[4] Some relevant

---

4 Nowadays in Artificial Intelligence as well there is great interest in programs that are able to "explain" in a transparent way the rationale of their output. This new research field, known as explainable AI or XAI, has begun to prosper after the huge commercial success of deep-learning based technologies, relying on the connectionist paradigm, and their usage in many fields, from autonomous driving to image and speech recognition, etc. Of course this aspect is

questions related to this issue include, among the others, the following: to what extent it is appropriate to say that a given artificial system (whose simulation and behaviour is used as a mean to provide an *explanans* – *"what explains something"*) has an explanatory role with respect to a phenomenon/behaviour of a natural system (the *explanandum* – *"what needs to be explained"*)? How can we compare different types of "cognitively inspired" systems (e.g., different types of *explanans*) trying to model the same phenomenon? And, at the end, which kind of explanation do we need in the context of cognitively inspired artificial systems?

Let's start with the latter question, since there are different views from the philosophy of science that are relevant in the context of cognitive modelling as well. First of all, intuitively, the notion of "explanation" is strictly linked to ones of causality and prediction. A good "explanation", whatever this term means, should be able to provide causal and predictive models of a certain phenomenon. However, different types of theories have been proposed to define what is a correct "explanation" from a scientific viewpoint (a recent reference dealing with an explanation and computational models of cognition is Minkowski, 2013). We will briefly review some of them, without pretending that there is any exhaustivity of this monumental topic here. The first type of theory about explanation is the so called Deductive-Nomological (DN) Explanation. According to this view, introduced by Hempel and Oppenheim (1948), there are some strict characteristics that an explanans have to satisfy in order to explain a given phenomenon (the explanandum). In particular, the explanandum is seen as something that needs to be logically derived, via deduction, from the explanans. While, intuitively, this theory adequately addresses a normative notion of explanation (since it assumes that the explanans provides the causes, i.e., the necessary and sufficient conditions, to understand the explanandum), such a requirement is very strict since there are many good explanations, in the scientific fields also, where the elements with an explanatory role (the explanans) are not able to completely "derive" a deductive account of the explanandum phenomenon (i.e., all empirical laws do not work in this way). DN Explanations, therefore, are impossible to obtain via empirical research done with computation models of cognition.[5] Other

---

also the most challenging one for neural nets due to their opacity (as we illustrated in the previous chapter, they work mainly as "black boxes"). On the other hand, logic- and symbol-based approaches seem to be more naturally suited to dealing with this kind of requirement. It is worth noting, however, that also symbolic approaches can be – to some extent – "opaque". This is the case, for example, with probabilistic semantic networks (as we will see in some detail in the next chapter through the example of the IBM Watson Question Answering System). In particular, in these cases, the opacity does not lie in the actual representation of the system but on how such representations are probabilistically connected among them.

5 There is also a probabilistic version of this theory but the key requirements of the DN explanation – that is, the facts that (i) the explanandum must be logically (deductively) derivable from the explanans, (ii) the explanans must contain at least a general law; (iii) the explanans must be empirically testable, and (iv) the explanans must be true – still hold. As may be evident from such requirements, the debate in the philosophy of science has mainly dealt with explanans intended as "scientific theories". In the use of computational tools for explanatory purposes all

explanatory theories developed in the literature concern so-called "teleological", "evolutionistic", and "mechanistic" explanations. We will briefly describe them by using a running example from the biological domain. Let us suppose that our aim is to explain the phenomenon according to which chameleons change their skin colour. This usually happens in the presence of a predator (they assume different colour configurations based on the predator they perceive) or potential mating partners. Now, if we are interested in an explanation about why chameleons assume more often the colour configuration associated with a particular predator (e.g., birds) a possible answer could be that "the number of bird predators is greater than the number of other animals and, thus, this has determined a stronger selective pressure". This is a typical example of an evolutionistic explanation, a type of explanation that plays an important role in many scientific theories. If we suppose, however, that the focus of our interest is just to understand why chameleons, in general, change their skin colour we could have other explanations. For example, a teleological explanation (from the Greek "*telos*", meaning scope) assumes that, in order to explain a phenomenon F one has to point out which is the ultimate scope that F allows one to achieve. In the example, if someone tells us that "chameleons change their skin colour to camouflage themselves and escape from predators", she simply provides an explanation about the scope of the phenomenon intended to explain. However, can we say that this kind of explanation helps us understand "why" chameleons change their colour? Of course this depends on the informative goal that we intend to satisfy with our question (i.e., what kind of "why" are we talking about) but, if we suppose that we are interested in the mechanisms that determine that phenomenon, we cannot really declare ourselves satisfied by that answer. On the other hand, if we receive the following explanation: "The skin colour change in chameleons is due to the response of some cells contained in the animal pigments (chromatophores) to nervous and endocrinous stimuli", we would probably be satisfied by this answer. In particular, our satisfaction would probably by derived from the fact that this kind of explanation shows the "mechanisms" that determine the phenomenon we want to understand. This kind of explanation is called "*mechanistic*" and represents the kind of explanation that is important to target when building artificial models of cognition. The crucial point in cognitive modelling, indeed, is exactly one of trying to build artificial artefacts able to shed light on the inner, unexplained mechanisms determining the behaviour of a given natural system. In the example provided, the very simple mechanistic explanation was also a causal explanation. However, in many cases, we are forced to use the so-called "inference to the best explanation" (IBE), i.e., a sort of empirically sound inductive/abductive procedure that can reasonably explain – given the state-of-the-art knowledge on a given phenomenon – certain mechanisms. Of course this may

---

these requirements, in particular the second and the fourth one, are impossible to adopt (since computational models are usually only partial instantiations of a particular theory and there is no absolute guarantee about the "logical truth" of the provided, if any, explanans).

also mean that there are explanatory theories of a given phenomenon that can turn out to be false. The scattering of alpha particles explained by Rutherford's theory of the atom or Lorentz's theory explaining clock retardation, for example, now are not thought to be true. In general, according to the IBE principle, it holds that, out of the class of potential explanations that we may have of some phenomenon, we should infer that the best explanation is the true one or the one that contextually seems to be "most true".[6]

In general, all these kinds of explanatory accounts can be useful in cognitive modelling and, since the investigated phenomena are complex ones, a wise move is to maintain an attitude of an "explicative pluralism" (even if, as we briefly have seen, mechanistic explanations seem to be the most important).

In order to further develop this "ecumenic" argument, let us consider with some additional detail the role of the above-mentioned teleological explanation. As the reader has probably already guessed, this kind of explanation assumes the ascription of some mental attitudes (and therefore the use of some "folk psychology" terms like "belief", "desire", and "goal") to the non-human system (either natural or, in our case, artificial) involved in the phenomenon one intends to explain. Indeed, if we assume an "intentional stance", to use Dennett's terminology that was introduced above, towards that system whose behaviour we aim to explain and predict, we are required to make exactly that ascription as an external observer. Now, why should we be interested in preserving this kind of observer-based explanation within a computationally grounded science of the mind? On this point, Valentino Braitenberg is clear when he warns,

> It is pleasurable and easy to create little machines that do certain tricks. It is also quite easy to observe the full repertoire of behaviour of these machines – even if it goes beyond what we originally planned – as it often does. But it is much more difficult to start from the outside and try to guess internal structure just from the observation of behaviour. It is actually impossible in theory to determine exactly what the hidden mechanisms [are] without opening the box, since there are always many different mechanisms with identical behavior. Quite apart from this, analysis is more difficult than invention in the sense in which, generally, invention takes

---

6 In this respect, a proponent of the contextual account of explanation like, Van Fraassen, claims, "A success of explanation is a success of adequate and informative description" (Van Fraassen, 1980: 156–157). It is worth noting that there are many other types of explanations (for example, the "functional account" proposed by Cunnings, where an explanation consists of providing "a function that a structure or system is believed to possess"). Such types of explanations are also useful but seem to be less relevant with respect to the aims of computational methods applied to the cognitive research agenda. To use the words of Piccinini (2007: 125): "Computational models that embody functional explanations explain the capacities of a system in terms of its sub-capacities. But this explanation is given by the assumptions embodied in the model, not by the computations performed by the model on the grounds of the assumptions."

more time to perform than deduction: in induction one has to search for the way whereas, in deduction, one follows a straightforward path.

(Braitenberg, 1986: 20)

So, why should we consider legitimate the use of a teleological explanation in a computational account of the study of the mind? The answer can be found, again, in the cybernetic tradition. Already by 1943, Rosenblueth, Wiener, and Bigelow had proposed in their famous paper, "Behavior, purpose and teleology", the inclusion of teleologic vocabulary to describe the behaviour of *feedback* machines (in particular those equipped with *negative feedback*[7]). In particular, they pointed out how it was justified to claim that certain classes of living organisms and machines have "purposeful" behaviour since their behaviour is teleologically guided by continuous (negative) feedback aimed at reaching a certain goal state. As a consequence, all the servomechanisms can display, to different degrees, teleological behaviour. In addition, it is worth noting that holding this kind of teleological "stance" can be considered a pragmatic option for the observer, and one that is justifiable if a system behaves as a rational agent and if there are not better, i.e., mechanistic, explanations available. As (Cordeschi, 2002) points out:

> If one considers the observer as model builder, we can see that his third-person viewpoint is the current one in scientific practice, where one constructs theories and models by selecting the functions believed to be essential to the phenomenon under study. The observer's role cannot be sidestepped, any more than the process of identifying hypothetical constructs in theory-building. As we have seen, models that include biological constraints are a priori no better or worse than models that include different constraints. These models identify functions like any other model, and it seems unlikely that identifying biological functions is per se more secure, more testable and, above all, less observer-relative than identifying other functions.
>
> *(265)*

After this rapid, and partial, overview of the different kinds of explanations, in the following section we will consider what we really mean when we talk about "cognitive/biological" plausibility and how this multifaceted element can be useful to determine a comparison between different types of artificial systems (cognitively inspired or not).

---

7 In the cybernetic tradition, machines capable of adapting themselves actively to the environment via trial-and-error processes based on negative feedback (used for autocorrection) were called "servomechanisms" or "negative feedback automata". An example of this type of machine is a radar-controlled cannon, where the radar provides constant information and feedback about a moving target (e.g., an airplane) so as to alter the gun's aim. This example should not surprise the reader, since research in cybernetics received a lot of impetus from World War II and its main early applications were in the military domain.

Levels of plausibility and the minimal cognitive grid (MCG)

Before introducing a pragmatic tool that can be useful in evaluating and comparing the explanatory levels of cognitively inspired systems, it is necessary to consider in greater detail the aspect of the different levels of "plausibility" that can be achieved in an artificial system. As mentioned in the previous chapter, an element that is worth considering in this respect concerns the irrelevance, with respect to the "plausibility" issue, of the level of abstraction adopted to model a given cognitive behaviour. In addition, it is worth noting that the notions of both cognitive and biological plausibility, in the context of computational Cognitive Science and computational modelling, refer to the level of accuracy obtained by the realization of an artificial system, with respect to the corresponding natural mechanisms (and their interactions) they are assumed to model. In particular, cognitive and biological plausibility of an artificial system asks for the development of artificial models (i) that are consistent (from a cognitive or biological point of view) with the current state-of-the-art knowledge about the modelled phenomenon and (ii) that adequately represent (at different levels of abstractions) the actual mechanisms operating in the target natural system and determining a certain behaviour.

Some of the key questions to answer in this respect are: what are the elements (e.g., the processes, the mechanisms, the structures, etc.) in the inspiring natural system that enable the rise of the desired behaviour? To what extent does the obtained behaviour depend on such elements? Definitive answers to these questions are still not available. However, in the context of biologically inspired artificial systems, different general criteria have been proposed to characterize the design of biologically plausible models. In this respect, the roboticist Barbara Webb (2001) identified a list of dimensions for the characterization of different design aspects of bio-inspired models. Here are the seven dimensions she identified:

1   **Biological relevance**: this dimension shows if, and eventually to what extent, a computational model can be used to generate and test hypotheses about a given biological system that is taken as a source of inspiration.
2   **Level**: this dimension aims at individuating "the basic elements of the model that have no internal structure or whose internal structures are ignored". In other words, it identifies the modelling focus. For example: an atomic model could be focused on the internal structures of atoms or could ignore this issue by focusing on the interactions between atoms (of course, the choice of the "level" also usually determines what class of formalisms can be adopted).
3   **Generality**: this feature aims at individuating how many different biological systems can be represented by a model.
4   **Abstraction**: this dimension considers how many details are included in the artificial model with respect to the natural system that is taken as a source of inspiration. According to Webb's terminology, "abstraction" should not be

confused with the "level" dimension. A more abstract model of a cognitive process could, indeed, contain more details and be more complex than the corresponding lower-level brain model of the same mechanism.

5   **Structural accuracy**: This feature intends to measure the similarity between the mechanisms behind the behaviour of an artificial model with respect to those of the target biological system. This aspect is directly affected by the state-of-the-art knowledge of the actual mechanisms in biological systems and is not necessarily proportional to how many details are included in the model.

6   **Performance match**: This dimension is intended to account for the similarity of the performances of the model with respect to the performances obtained by the target biological system.

7   **Medium**: this dimension refers to the physical medium used to implement the model.

Despite the huge influence of Webb's characterization of the dimensions to take into account when designing and evaluating bio-inspired systems, however, this proposal is limited in a number of ways. First, it explicitly targets biologically plausible constraints. It does not consider, for example, different types of higher-level cognitive constraints that one could indeed consider in a "plausible" model of human (or natural) cognition. In addition, it does not consider non-embodied agents/simulations, thus neglecting a huge class of models developed within the cognitive modelling and AI communities. Furthermore, some dimensions do not appear to be self-explanatory. For example, the concepts of "biological relevance" or "structural accuracy" are highly overlapping and there is no clearly defined method that one could use to determine how such elements are/can be operationally defined. Similarly the concept of "medium" is assumed to consider the physical instantiation carrying out the computations of the computational model and is evidently related to the physical level in Marr's hierarchy (described in the previous chapter). However, the Webb proposal explicitly limits the considerations on this aspect to the presence (or lack thereof) of an embodied agent. The "medium", in her view, is the physical body of the agent (a robot). This view is, however, quite restrictive since it does not consider, for example, alternative physical models of computations based on quantum computers or hybrid biological/artificial neural networks realized in the field of neuromorphing computing.

   In the following section, I propose a much more synthetic list of elements that subsumes some of Webb's dimensions and that, additionally, can be applied not only to biologically inspired systems but also to cognitively inspired ones. This latter aspect is important since, as we saw in the previous chapter, artificial plausibility can be obtained at different levels of abstractions (not only at the neurophysiological or biological level), using different formalisms and modelling approaches. In addition, the proposed characterization has the merit of providing a set of characteristics that can be directly used to compare different biologically or cognitively inspired systems and as a tool to project their explanatory power.

The proposed minimal set of analytic dimensions to consider, which I call the "Minimal Cognitive Grid" (MCG), comprises the following aspects:

1 **Functional/Structural Ratio**: this dimension concerns the individuation of the elements upon which the artificial model/system is built. For example, in a complex artificial system (embodied or not) it is possible to model, in a "functional" way, some elements of the system whose internal structure and mechanisms are not considered important with respect to one's explanatory goals and, on the other hand, it is possible to build structural models of other components of the same system. In other words, this dimension looks at the ratio between functional and structural components (and heuristics) considered in the design and implementation of an artificial system. This ratio depends on the actual focus and goal of the model and can be used for both integrated systems performing different types of tasks and for narrow and task-specific systems. This dimension synthesizes and subsumes the "biological relevance" and "structural accuracy" individuated by Webb by enabling, in principle, the possibility of performing both a quantitative and qualitative comparison between different artificial systems (whether they are cognitively inspired or not). Of course, in this case, the lower the ratio, the better. The "system dissection" required by this dimension of analysis is also useful to individuate the kind of explanations that can be ascribed to different components of the systems (e.g., a mechanistic explanation would make sense only for the "structurally modelled" components).

2 **Generality**: as in the Webb proposal, this feature aims at evaluating to what extent a given system/architecture can be used in different tasks, i.e., how general is the model and whether it can be used to simulate a set of cognitive functions and not just a narrow one. Also this element can be considered both from a quantitative (e.g., by counting how many cognitive faculties can be modelled within a single system) and qualitative point of view.

3 **Performance Match**: as in the Webb proposal, this dimension involves a direct comparison between natural and artificial systems in terms of the obtained results for specific or general tasks. With respect to Webb's account, however, I propose a more precise characterization of this dimension when we consider human beings the "natural system" used as a reference point. In particular, I suggest taking into account some of the main hints of the *Psychometric AI* movement (Bringsjord, 2011) that asks for the use of a battery of validated tests to assess the effective "match" between artificial systems and human beings. Along this line, thus, I also propose considering two additional specific requirements that refer to such an aspect: (1) the analysis of system errors (which, in human-like artificial systems, should be similar to those committed by humans) and (2) the execution time of the tasks (which, again, should converge towards human performances). Therefore, in this configuration, the degree of accuracy obtained in certain performances is not sufficient to claim any kind of biological or cognitive plausibility. Of

course, the inclusion of the two additional requirements (if considered in isolation) similarly does not guarantee any plausibility claim (since a system could match these additional psychometric measures without being a "structural model"). However, it is worth noting that all three dimensions conceived for the MCG, considered together, can provide an objective evaluation of the structural accuracy of a model. As with the first two dimensions, the rating assumed on the third dimension can be also, in principle, determined with both quantitative (e.g., by considering the difference in terms of results, errors, and execution times between the natural and artificial systems) or qualitative means.

In qua descriptors of the "structural accuracy" of a given system, the MCG dimensions allow the *de facto* operationalization of the x-axis on the *Enriched 2D Space of Cognitive Systems*.

A further dimension of analysis, not included in the MCG but one that could be useful to consider, is the "modelling paradigm" adopted in the development of a given system (this dimension only partially overlaps with the "level" dimension in Barbara Webb's account). Such a criterion, however, does not lie on the same ground as the previous ones, since it does not play any role in regards to the individuation of the structural adequacy and the explanatory capability of the analyzed systems. On the other hand, it can be useful as a qualitative dimension to analyze the commitments (if any) of systems adopting different modelling paradigms (symbolic, hybrid, and connectionist) to the cognitive research agenda.

Summing up: by starting from the original proposal from Barbara Webb, we have individuated a minimal set of dimensions (which we have called the "Minimal Cognitive Grid") that can be used as an analytical tool to compare different kinds of cognitive artificial systems and their degree of structural accuracy with respect to human performances and abilities. This tool is general enough to include both biological and cognitive modelling approaches and allows a comparison between them in terms of their explanatory capacity with respect to the natural system that is taken as source of inspiration.

4

EXAMPLES OF COGNITIVELY INSPIRED SYSTEMS AND APPLICATION OF THE MINIMAL COGNITIVE GRID

Abstract

Given the proposal presented in the book so far, this chapter describes some practical applications of the Minimal Cognitive Grid by showing how it allows one to collocate different types of artificial systems in the landscape formed by the cognitive design approach. Examples of artificial models of cognition and cognitive architectures will be presented and compared with examples of functionalist AI systems that, despite being called instances of "cognitive computing", cannot be considered realistic models of our cognition.

Modern AI systems: cognitive computing?

As sketched out in the first chapter, Artificial Intelligence (AI) is nowadays mainly focused on building systems able to execute, in an efficient and efficacious way, specialized tasks in a variety of domains, ranging from machine translation to autonomous cars and robotics. Also the two most successful AI systems of the last decade, namely IBM Watson (Ferrucci et al., 2013) and the Alpha Go System (Silver et al., 2017) developed by Google, can indeed be assigned to the category of narrow AI systems. In addition to the being narrow, however, they have another important quality: they are "Super-Human" AI systems. "Super-Human" because they have outperformed humans in two different complex tasks like question answering (Watson) and *Go* (Alpha Go), a popular strategic game – mostly known in Asia – that is much more complex than chess from the point of view of the combinatory explosion of possible moves.

Let's explore the details: the Watson question-answering system was able to defeat human champions of a game known as *Jeopardy!* (a very famous TV quiz show in the USA, consisting of answering rich natural language questions covering a broad range of general knowledge) by integrating several AI techniques that mainly resort to probabilistic strategies for the determination of its output. In the original version of *Jeopardy!* there are three human contestants. The game in which Watson successfully participated consisted of two human players plus the IBM system.

Alpha Go, on the other hand, is a deep neural network system incorporating *reinforcement learning strategies* (i.e., strategies similar to the "operant conditioning" adopted in the *behaviourist* tradition of psychology and described in the previous chapters, see footnote 17 in Chapter 1) that defeated the human world champion of *Go*: the South Korean Lee Seidol. Such system has been developed by Deep Mind, an innovative spin-off company from Google, specializing in the development of novel deep learning techniques. Alpha Go achieved such results after being trained for several thousands of hours on previous games played by human champions of *Go*. It relied on a Monte Carlo Tree Search (MTCS)[1] strategy and on two different specialized deep neural networks using reinforcement learning. These two networks are a *policy network*, deciding what move to make, and a *value network* that analyzes the position of the pieces on the board.[2]

Such systems are important for the purposes of this book since they constitute a recent example of inappropriate labelling coming from the "cognitive" vocabulary and ascribed to successful AI systems. These systems, indeed, have been often claimed in these years, both in the media and in scientific AI conferences, to be member of the class of "cognitive computing" systems. This attribution has been usually justified in light of the impressive results obtained and, in the case of the Watson system, due to its ability to deal with questions in natural language. However, as already mentioned in Chapter 2 and as should be clearer at this point of the book, this qualification is incorrect and misleading since these system have been built according to a "functional" approach and without any cognitive constraint able to justify the expression "cognitive computing" attached to them. In other words, these systems do not have any explanatory role with respect to the analogous human functions that they aim to replicate. This "new story" is actually not so new in its development. In particular, if we look back at the case of the IBM chess machine Deep Blue, which in 1997 defeated the then chess World Champion Garry Kasparov by exploiting its computational strengths (e.g., in particular its memory storage capacity and, among other sophisticated

---

1 Monte Carlo Tree Search (MTCS) is a strategy for obtaining optimal decisions and one that is adopted in a variety of AI applications. In the context of *Go*, the game is represented as a tree (a game tree). With this problem configuration, MCTS is able to assign to each node of the game tree a statistical value that highlights the most interesting nodes in the tree (thus avoiding the combinatorial explosion of possible moves). The values are assigned by simulations (that start randomly and are later adjusted via backward updates). In the context of *Go* MTCS plays a role similar to the one played by the so-called "*minimax* algorithms" (see below) in the game of chess.

2 Its successor, Alpha Go Zero, introduced some architectural novelty (e.g., the combination of the two neural networks in a huge larger one) as well as the capability of learning from self-play rather than from a huge training set represented by thousands of hours of expert games.

technicalities, the *minimax algorithm*[3] to decide its next move), we have a similar situation: the result obtained by the system was impressive from an AI perspective but was not particularly significant from the point of view of psychological realism of the simulation. Nonetheless, the understandable enthusiasm for this impressive achievement similarly risked leading to improper ascriptions of other super "intelligent" faculties to the IBM program. Of course, the fact that such new AI systems, in the same way as Deep Blue, cannot be defined as "cognitive systems" or "cognitive computing systems" is not a *diminutio* from a technological or engineering point of view since – as stated from the beginning – they represent the state of the art in their respective fields and are very sophisticated AI technologies. However, the sloppy and propagandistic attribution of expressions coming from the "cognitive science" vocabulary to AI systems legitimately adopting "machine-oriented" heuristic solutions/approaches to solve problems, is a source of conceptual confusion not only among non-AI experts but also within the AI community itself.[4]

Given this clarification, let us "test" the Minimal Cognitive Grid presented above on these two systems. The first point concerns the *functional/structural ratio* of the proposed model. In both cases, there is no structural constraint that has been assumed about mental or brain processes. Therefore, on this aspect such systems are completely functional. From a *generality* perspective both systems are task specific: Watson can do Question Answering and not, for example, Machine Translation or Computer Vision tasks. Similarly, the architecture of Alpha Go (and of its successor *Alpha Go Zero*) can learn play to *Go* and can't do other tasks. It is worth noting, however, that a generalization of the two original versions of the Alpha Go architecture – called *Alpha Zero* – has been successfully able to learn, at a super-human level, other similar, *Go*-related board games like chess and *shogi* (a strategic game very famous in Japan). All these games, however, are very similar in nature, although they have a different degree of complexity (with *Go* being the most complex one and, thus, in a certain sense, already "subsuming" the other two games). As a consequence, the classical *transfer learning* problem

---

3 The minimax is a decision procedure used to minimise the loss function in a worst-case scenario. Similarly to the MCTS, this procedure – when applied to the chess game – establishes at each node of the game (also formalized as a "tree") which branch leads to a position of maximum advantage for system and minimum advantage for his adversary. Of course this evaluation cannot be done on the whole "game tree" via "brute force" algorithms (since this leads to a combinatorial explosion) and different "bounds" can be applied. Deep Blue, for example, was able to "see" and apply this procedure from 12 to 40 turns ahead with respect to the current situation in the game (see, Hsu and Feng-Hsiung, 1999). Kasparov, of course, did not have this possibility.

4 Anecdotal facts are not scientifically relevant and there is no exception here. However, sometimes they can help give an idea of the state of affairs. Personally, I remember at least a couple of recent occasions, one at the International Joint Conference on Artificial Intelligence with a very famous researcher in NLP, and another one during a "Cognitive Computing Symposium" organised at ESCOP 2015 (sponsored by IBM Research, to which I was kindly invited by Antonis Kakas, Loizos Michael, and Irene-Anna Diakidoy) where I expressed these basic concerns and my words came as a surprise to some (too many) researchers in the audience (including those from IBM).

affecting deep net architectures – and concerning the fact that the models learnt by these architectures are task specific and are not able to be generalized to other problems – remains unanswered.

In regards to the last point of our Minimal Cognitive Grid, the *performance match*, these systems have achieved, as mentioned, super-human performances. So at first glance, it seems that they perform very well on this dimension. As mentioned before, however, the performance match dimension, in order to be relevant from a biological/cognitive perspective, should consider both success and error cases. Since the successes of both systems are well known and have been described above, let us focus on some of the errors produced by them. Upon closer look it appears that both these systems, or better: their underlying technological solutions, have produced – in some cases – very strange and "sub-human" errors. "Sub-human" since no one, including seven to eight year old children, would have produced the kind of errors that the underlying architectures of such systems have provided in certain situations. Let us look in more detail at what these "errors" look like: the very famous case involving the Watson system during its *Jeopardy!* match against the two human champions is what we can call the "Toronto dilemma". In particular, during the game, one of the questions proposed to both the system and the two humans was, "What is the US city whose largest airport is named after a World War II hero and whose second largest airport after a World War II Battle?"[5] While the human champions quite easily provided the correct answer, "Chicago", the response provided by the probabilistic engine of Watson was, incredibly, "Toronto". Now, it is not necessary to be a *Jeopardy!* champion to know that Toronto is not a US city! IBM engineers tried for months to understand what triggered that answer and why Watson replied in that way but were unsuccessful – this is an example of how "opacity" is also a feature of probabilistic symbolic systems.

Let us consider now the Alpha Go system. For this system there is no direct report of a similar non-human failure during its matches against Lee Seidol. From this point of view, however, it should be noted that dealing with language risks a greater probability of the kind of errors presented above since understanding language is a more complicated task than playing a table game, even if it is a complex one like *Go*. It involves, indeed, a plethora of different complex subproblems (from anaphora resolution to semantic ambiguity, etc.) that do not have a definitive solution in the context of natural language processing. In the context of *Go*, on the other hand, it is also difficult for humans to evaluate eventual erroneous moves played by the system since the strategies employed are not interpretable from our perspective. As a matter of fact, the learning strategies of the Alpha Go system and its successors showed a better modelling capability of the task environment (i.e., the board of the game and the different positioning patterns

---

5 The video of this moment of the *Jeopardy!* game is also available on YouTube: https://www.youtube.com/watch?v=Y2wQQ-xSE4s&t=3s.

of the pieces at each point in time). The "acquired" knowledge about their environment, a crucial element for the exhibition of intelligent behaviour as showed in Simon's ant metaphor, included the analysis of different "optimal patterns" on the whole board. This global view enabled the system to explore unknown positioning patterns (i.e., there were moves and situations never played by any human player) and to find, also in these situations, optimal decision strategies. Another interesting finding that came from the analysis of the Alpha Go results is that this system was somehow able to treat what is considered a strategic reasoning game as a vision game: the use of the so called convolutional networks – a particular type of deep networks mainly used in computer vision and adopted in Alpha Go architecture in both the "policy" and "value" networks – for the correct identification and categorization of different game patterns is paradigmatic in this respect.

It is exactly from this strength, however, that potential risks for systems like Go and other deep learning systems (including autonomous cars) also arise. Convolutional neural networks, indeed, raised many criticisms when, upon being applied to an image recognition task in a Google Photo application, mislabelled a black couple as gorillas,[6] an incomprehensible error to the human eye. Additionally, it has been subsequently demonstrated how it is relatively easy to deliberately fool these networks by using "adversarial networks" (another class of deep nets that are able to learn what minimal set of pixels to change in order to let the attacked network generate a wrong classification with respect to the original, correct one). In particular, a study by Su et al. (2017) showed how, in certain cases, a single pixel change could lead to completely diverse categorizations (the study shows, for example, how picture originally labelled as "Egyptian cat" was successively classified as a "bath towel"; similarly, a "giant panda" was later classified as a "vulture"). Of course these single-pixel changes are invisible to the human visual system and, as such, this kind of "sub-human" error is symptomatic of the fact that – as in the case of Watson – the underlying components of the Alpha Go system (and therefore the system as a whole) cannot be qualified as structural models.

To sum up: by applying our Minimal Cognitive Grid as a tool to analyze the two systems, it becomes evident why they both cannot be considered cognitive systems. They are actually two admirable examples of functional AIs that make no structural assumptions. In regards to the generality criterion: at first glance, Alpha Go (and, in particular, its successor Alpha Zero) seems to perform better that Watson on this dimension. But that's only an illusion. As mentioned, in fact, the "transfer" towards other games was obtained for board games that, in nature, were of the same type as *Go* but less complex (and, as such, were somehow "subsumed" by the kind of strategies put in place for *Go* itself). In other words, if

---

6 As reported by the *MIT Technology Review* in November 2018, the strategy used by Google to "fix" this problem has been one of censoring image tags relating to many primates https://www.technologyreview.com/2018/01/11/146257/google-photos-still-has-a-problem-with-gorillas/.

Watson would have been successfully applied to the famous game *Who wants to be a millionaire?* as well, presenting different simplifications with respect to *Jeopardy!*, we similarly would not have taken that as evidence of a more general capability of that system.

With reference to the performance: both the underlying architectures adopted by the two systems have shown super-human strengths and sub-human limitations. Therefore, even if it is true that in Watson such limitations were "directly" manifested during the game and in the case of Alpha Go they were only "indirectly" shown through the functionality of its core components used in other applications, from the analysis of their types of errors it seems evident that both these systems cannot play any kind of explanatory role with respect to the corresponding human cognitive mechanisms they model in an AI setting.

In the following section, we will explore a completely different kind of artificial system, one we briefly mentioned in the first chapter of the book: the cognitive architectures.

Cognitive architectures

The term "cognitive architecture" was introduced by Allen Newell (1990) that, starting from the 1980s, initiated his own research agenda looking for Unified Theories of Cognition to be realized via integrated intelligent systems. This view diverged from that of his historical colleague Herbert Simon, who, instead, continued in his efforts of building computational micro-models of specific cognitive phenomena. For Newell, on the other hand, it was starting to be clear that "you can't play 20 questions with nature and win" (as the title of his famous 1973 cognitive science paper had already suggested). So he started to work on the notion of cognitive architectures that, in Newell's view, should have played the same "middleware-like" role that computer architectures do with respect to the underlying hardware implementations and the top software layers whose interactions and information processing mechanisms they regulate.

To look at this more in detail: this class of artificial systems was described, in a recent editorial on the subject published in the journal *Cognitive Systems Research* that I co-authored with Mehul Bhatt, Alessandro Oltramari, and David Vernon, as follows:

> Cognitive Architectures indicate both abstract models of cognition, in natural and artificial agents, and the software instantiations of such models which are then employed in the field of Artificial Intelligence (AI). The main role of Cognitive Architectures in AI is that one of enabling the realization of artificial systems able to exhibit intelligent behavior in a general setting through a detailed analogy with the constitutive and developmental functioning and mechanisms underlying human cognition. The research on Cognitive Architectures (CAs), in particular, is a wide and active area involving a plethora of disciplines such as Cognitive Science,

Artificial Intelligence, Robotics and, more recently, the area of Computational Neuroscience. CAs have been historically introduced (i) "to capture, at the computational level, the invariant mechanisms of human cognition, including those underlying the functions of control, learning, memory, adaptivity, perception and action" (this goal is crucial in the cognitivist perspective (ii) to form the basis for the development of cognitive capabilities through ontogeny over extended periods of time (this goal is one of the main target of the so called emergent perspective), (iii) to reach human level intelligence, also called General Artificial Intelligence, by means of the realization of artificial artifacts built upon them.

Lieto, Bhatt, Oltramari and Vernon (2018: 1–2)

The characterization above shows how this class of system aims at building structural models, or artificial models of cognition, that are also expected to be state-of-the-art artificial systems according to cognitive-AI assumptions. What also emerges from the definition above is that the emergentist vs. cognitivist dichotomy is also reflected in this sub-area of AI and cognitive modelling research. During the last few decades, many cognitive architectures have been built relying on different theoretical and practical assumptions.

A recent survey by Kotsteruba and Tsotsos (2020) points out how over the last 40 years more than 80 different Cognitive Architectures (developed in both in their theoretical and computational counterparts and adopting cognitivist, emergentist, and hybrid approaches) have been proposed, tested, and maintained. This underlines the role that such computational artefacts have played in the past, by relying on different inspiring principles as simulative tools for understanding the mind and the underlying dynamics and interconnections between its processing mechanisms. As the computational cognitive scientist Ron Sun correctly pointed out, cognitive architectures

play an important role in computational modeling of cognition in that they make explicit the set of assumptions upon which that cognitive model is founded. These assumptions are typically derived from several sources: biological or psychological data, philosophical arguments, or ad hoc working hypotheses inspired by work in different disciplines such as neurophysiology, psychology, or artificial intelligence. Once it has been created, a cognitive architecture also provides a framework for developing the ideas and assumptions encapsulated in the architecture.

(Sun, 2004)

Interestingly enough, Sun points out an important aspect of cognitive architecture research that we will see in greater detail in the following sections: namely the fact that the general structural requirements of cognitive architecture need to be tested on specialized computational models (e.g., of reasoning, selective attention, categorization, etc.) built within those architectural constraints. It is the simulation run on such specific computational models, built in compliance with the general architectural assumptions of a cognitive architecture, that provides insights about the plausibility/implausibility of the modelled mechanisms.

Along with the different implementations and software instantiations developed in the last few decades, many different requirements and desiderata have been proposed in order to build integrated cognitive systems of this type. For example, on the "cognitivist" side, Langley, Laird, and Rogers (2009) individuated the following abilities that such systems should be capable of performing (by exploiting different task-specific models) and integrating by using the same underlying architectural assumptions:

1   Recognition and categorization
2   Decision-making and choice
3   Perception and situation assessment
4   Prediction and monitoring
5   Problem solving and planning
6   Reasoning and belief maintenance
7   Execution and action
8   Interaction and communication
9   Remembering, reflection, and learning

Also, Ron Sun identified four desirable features of a cognitive architecture. These are: ecological realism; bio-evolutionary realism; cognitive realism; and eclecticism of methodologies and techniques. These can be described as follows: the first one concerns the idea that a cognitive architecture should focus on allowing the artificial cognitive system to operate in its natural environment, engaging in "everyday activities" (Sun, 2004) and, as such, should be able to perceive, decide among conflicting goals, etc. Bio-evolutionary realism postulates that a cognitive model of human intelligence should be reducible to a model of animal intelligence since human intelligence evolved from the capabilities of earlier primates. The cognitive realism principle postulates the necessity of building what we have defined as "structural models".[7] The last feature, finally, points out the necessity of assuming a pluralistic perspective in regards to the modelling methodologies and techniques to use; and suggest that new models should draw on, subsume, or supersede older models.

---

7 As concerns cognitive realism, Sun underlines the role of implicit and explicit processes (directly reflected in its own cognitive architecture: CLARION [Sun, 2007]). In particular, he posits that the interconnection between such different processes should encompass all the cognitive faculties (from learning to reasoning to metacognition). In the CLARION cognitive architecture (Sun, 2007), implicit processes operate on connectionist representations and explicit processes on symbolic representations. This architecture is an example of a hybrid architecture able to affect autonomous generation of explicit conceptual structures by exploiting implicit knowledge acquired by trial-and-error learning, and it can also affect top-down learning by integrating externally provided knowledge in the form of explicit rule-based conceptual structures and assimilating these into the bottom-level implicit representation.

More recently, Vernon et al. (2017) proposed a set of desiderata for emergentist and developmental cognitive architectures, focusing on partially different cognitive faculties with respect to those proposed by Langley and the cognitivist researchers. In particular, in this perspective, the most important aspects concern the capability of an agent of learning via physical, embodied, perceptual interaction with the environment, what actions to take and, in general, what principles to put in place in order to replicate the developmental ontogenetic capacities of humans within a cognitive architecture. Cognitive architectures, therefore, are assumed to represent the overall infrastructure resulting from the phylogenetic development of an organism and from which intelligent action and decisions should develop. Along this line, Vernon and colleagues identify ten desiderata for the design and development of such types of architecture:

1 the need of having a *value system* able to guide the selection of actions to take;
2 the need of having a *physical embodiment* (which is not considered a necessity for the cognitivist agenda);
3 the need to implement the capacity of learning *sensorimotor contingencies*; i.e., "the relation between the actions that the agent performs and the change it experiences in its sensed data because of those actions" (Vernon et al., 2017);
4 the need for a developed *perceptual apparatus*, with a variety of physical sensory and motor interfaces to allow the system to act on the world and perceive the effects of these actions. – the richer the sensorimotor interface, the richer the model of the world the agent can construct –
5 the need to implement *attentional mechanisms* for facilitating cognitive development;
6 the need for subsystems able to deal with the capability of *prospective action* (i.e., goal-directed actions guided by prospection and triggered by values);
7 the need to distinguish, in the memory system of the architecture, between *declarative* and *procedural memory,* which respectively store the "knowing that" and the "knowing how" learned;
8 the need to integrate different types of *learning strategies*: supervised learning (i.e., the types of learning based on a supervised training based on previous examples, like the one seen in Alpha Go), reinforcement learning, and unsupervised learning (the type of learning obtained with no human supervision);
9 the need to model effects able to generate *internal simulations* in the model; and
10 the need to develop systems with a *constitutive autonomy* based on internal self-organization able to maintain the agent's organizational parameters within operational bounds.

One of the most relevant outcomes of this emergentist and embodied perspective is represented by the iCub cognitive architecture (Metta et al., 2010), developed by Giulio Sandini, Giorgio Metta, and their group at IIT (the Italian Institute of Technology) and employed in the humanoid robot iCub. As Vernon also points out (Vernon, 2014), however, while this class of embodied cognitive architectures has shown interesting performances for perceptual-related tasks, ontogenetic learning (including language acquisition, see Cangelosi and Parisi, 2012), and sensorimotor coordination, there is currently still a gap with respect to the older cognitive architectures developed within the cognitivist and the hybrid traditions that have been used in a wider variety of tasks, partially overlapping with the lower level activities of emergentist architectures but, additionally, resulting in more convincing performances and structural accuracy for tasks concerning high-level cognitive faculties and going from reasoning, to natural language understanding, to planning and meta-level cognitive capabilities.

Currently, among the many different cognitive architectures realized, the two unanimously recognized as the most successful ones in the AI and cognitive modelling communities are, without any doubt, SOAR and ACT-R, widely tested in several cognitive tasks involving learning, multi-step reasoning, selective attention, multimodal perception, recognition, and many others. In the following section, we first provide a general overview of both of these architectures by illustrating their main, general structural elements. Furthermore, in order to actually compare the structural accuracy and explanatory power of such systems, we will focus on a specific type of computational models dealing with the process of conceptual categorization and retrieval: a task I have worked on extensively over the last decade.

SOAR

SOAR (Laird, 2012) is the oldest cognitive architecture developed (see Figure 4.1 for an overview). Originally the name coined by Newell and his colleagues was an acronym for **S**tate **O**perate **A**nd **R**esult, which synthesized its main theme: the fact that all cognitive tasks are represented by symbolic problem spaces containing a series of states. Such spaces are searched by production rules grouped into operators. This heuristic search driven behaviour was inherited directly from the GPS system. Exactly as in the GPS, SOAR indeed accomplishes problem solving by selecting, given a certain goal state to reach, appropriate operators able to reduce the "symbolic distance" between the goal state and current state. In addition, SOAR was directly inspired by the cognitive psychology research for its memory system, which distinguishes between a Long-Term Memory – nowadays composed of a Semantic Memory and an Episodic Memory (storing information about facts) and a Procedural Memory (storing knowledge as production rules; i.e., rules of the type "if x then Y") – and a Working Memory, also known as Short-Term Memory and used as a sort of buffer for the temporary and "short term" storage of the knowledge to handle while performing a given task. The production rules are read in parallel to producing reasoning cycles. From a representational perspective, SOAR exploits symbolic representations of knowledge (called "chunks") and uses pattern matching to select relevant knowledge elements. SOAR activity is based on a decision cycle: given a goal to reach, when a production matches the contents of the working memory, the rule fires and the knowledge stored in one

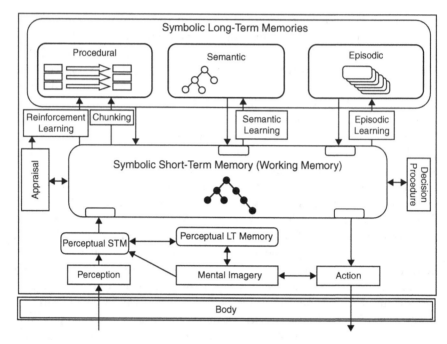

FIGURE 4.1 The SOAR cognitive architecture, from Laird (2012), with permission from MIT Press.

of the two declarative memories (Semantic or Episodic) is retrieved. In the cases where SOAR cannot proceed with the selection of the appropriate operator to solve the goal, it reaches a so-called *impasse:* a core notion in the SOAR architecture representing a trigger for learning. In particular, when an impasse arises in SOAR, the system recalibrates itself by assuming a new goal: the resolution of the impasse. In this way, the new goal (i.e., the solution of the impasse) becomes a subgoal of the original one (the whole process is known as *universal subgoaling*) and the original goal is returned to only once the subgoal is achieved and the impasse resolved. Learning in SOAR is strongly dependent on the subgoaling process. Indeed, whenever a subgoal has been achieved, the resolution procedure that has led to that achievement is added to the knowledge base to prevent the impasse that produced the subgoal from occurring again (this learning process is known as *chunking*). If an impasse occurs because the consequences of an operator are unknown, and in the subgoal these consequences are subsequently found, knowledge is added to SOAR's memory about the consequences of that operator. An additional feature of the architecture concerns the possibility of using external inputs to extend its Semantic Memory. Such knowledge can be used to solve the impasse and can be incorporated into the learned rules. A crucial connection with cognitive constraints in SOAR, apart from the assumptions about the memory system and the heuristic search hypothesis, is represented by the strict connection between its internal information processing mechanisms and the so-called "Newell's time scales of human action" (see Table 4.1).

TABLE 4.1 Newell's timescale of human actions

Band	Scale (sec)	Time units	System
Social	10^7	Months	
	10^5	Weeks	
	10^5	Days	
Rational	10^4	Hours	Task
	10^3	10 minutes	Task
	10^2	Minutes	Task
Cognitive	10^1	10 seconds	Unit task
	10^0	1 second	Operations
	10^{-1}	100 ms	Deliberate act
Biological	10^{-2}	10 ms	Neural circuit
	10^{-3}	1 ms	Neuron
	10^{-4}	100 μs	Organelle

Newell (1990).

This time scale was proposed by Newell (1990) as an important element for understanding cognitive behaviour. In particular, the underlying assumption of Newell's time scale is that there are regularities at these different time scales (each corresponding to different "bands" of behaviour) that can be studied somewhat independently of the time scales above and below them. SOAR processes have a high mapping with the timing individuated in Newell's time scale (Table 4.1).

ACT-R

ACT-R (Anderson et al., 2004) is a cognitive architectures explicitly inspired by theories and experimental results coming from human cognition and, just like SOAR, is a candidate architecture for providing a unified theory of cognition. The website (http://act-r.psy.cmu.edu) counts hundreds of models developed for a huge variety of tasks. ACT-R is nowadays considered a hybrid architecture (whereas it originally started as a symbolic one) since it couples sub-symbolic processing and symbolic ones. This architecture is composed of four main modules and a production system: (a) a visual module for identifying objects in the visual field, (b) a goal module for keeping track of current goals and intentions, (c) a declarative module for the storage and retrieval of information from memory, and (d) a manual module for controlling the motor commons of robotic hands (real or simulated). The core control component of the ACT-R cognitive architecture is represented by the central production memory that connects all the ACT-R subsystems, in particular the working memory modules – implemented as specialized buffers – by using a set of IF-THEN production rules. As with SOAR, ACT-R also distinguishes between different types of memory: a declarative long-term memory (which is not additionally divided into specific sub-memories), a working memory (or better: a set of working memories represented by different buffers used to communicate with the different modules of the architecture), and, as mentioned, a central procedural memory that stores knowledge as production rules and is internally responsible for three sub-operations like "rule matching", "rule selection", and "rule execution" (see Figure 4.2). In ACT-R, the cognitive mechanisms concerning knowledge processing emerge from the interaction of two types of knowledge: declarative knowledge, which encodes explicit facts that the system knows, and procedural knowledge, which encodes rules for processing declarative knowledge. In particular, the declarative module is used to store and retrieve pieces of information (called "chunks", composed of a type and a set of attribute-value pairs, similar to frame slots) in declarative memory. As mentioned, ACT-R employs a wide range of sub-symbolic processes for the activation of symbolic conceptual chunks representing the encoded knowledge. In particular, chunks are made available in the working memory buffers to the degree that past experiences indicate that they will be useful at the particular

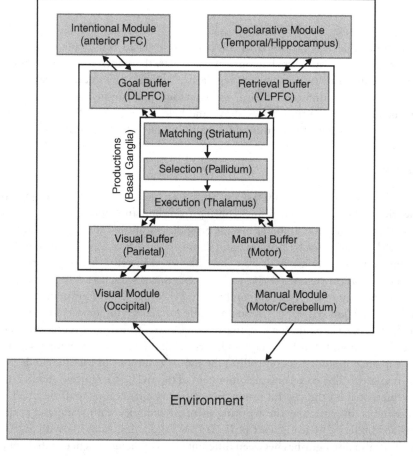

FIGURE 4.2 The ACT-R cognitive architecture (permission from Elsevier).

moment and the chunk activation strategy relies upon a number of parameters that are in line with the Rational Analysis hypothesis by John Anderson (who is also the developer of the ACT-R theory). Differing from SOAR, which is more oriented towards AI applications, ACT-R is more constrained with experimental data coming from psychological and neuroscientific experiments. For example: as the Figure 4.2 indicates, the different kind of processes operated in ACT-R have been explicitly mapped to processes activated in specific brain regions (represented in round parenthesis in the figure). In addition, ACT-R has limited buffer capacities for the processing mechanisms of its Working Memory (or Short-Term Memory). This aspect is compliant with well-known work done by the psychologist G.A. Miller (Miller, 1956), who showed that the short-term human memory has a capacity of about seven distinct elements (in this regard, Miller speaks of the «magical number seven plus or minus two»). On the other hand, working memory processing is unconstrained in SOAR.

In order to actually compare the structural accuracy and explanatory power of both ACT-R and SOAR, we will not consider the entire range of models developed upon them in the last few decades since this attempt would probably require an entire book on its own. On the contrary, we will focus on a specific type of computational model dealing with the process of categorization and retrieval. This reductionist choice allows us to focus on specific mechanisms, making it easier to understand the application of the "Minimal Cognitive Grid" as a tool for the analysis of cognitive artificial systems.

Two problems for the knowledge level in cognitive architectures

Before delving into our case study, it is necessary to introduce the current context of the problem that we are going to analyze. In a recent article I co-authored with Christian Lebiere (one of the main ACT-R developers) and Alessandro Oltramari, entitled "The knowledge level in cognitive architectures: Current limitations and possible developments" (Lieto, Lebiere, and Oltramari, 2018), we pointed out how Cognitive Architectures, in order to play an epistemological and explanatory role, in regards to their knowledge processing capabilities, had to face two main issues: the *limited size* and the *homogeneous typology* of the encoded and processed knowledge. These two problems emerged from a knowledge level analysis (*à la* Newell) of the capabilities of such systems. In particular, we pointed out how – concerning the size problem – the

> knowledge embedded and processed in such architectures is usually very
> limited, ad-hoc built, domain specific, or based on the specific tasks they
> have to deal with. Thus, every evaluation of the artificial systems relying
> upon them, is necessarily task-specific and do not involve not even the
> minimum part of the full spectrum of processes involved in the human
> cognition when the "knowledge" comes to play a role. As a consequence,
> the structural mechanisms that the CAs implement concerning knowledge

processing tasks (e.g., that ones of retrieval, learning, reasoning, etc.) can be only loosely evaluated, and compared w.r.t. that ones used by humans in similar knowledge-intensive situations.

(2)

In other words, we posited that, from an epistemological perspective, the explanatory power of their computational simulation was strongly affected. In reference to the problem of the "homogeneous typology" of the encoded knowledge, on the other hand, we pointed out that the current versions of the cognitive architectures did not consider some important theoretical and experimental results coming from Cognitive Science concerning the nature of the different types of conceptual representations and the different types of reasoning and categorization procedures associated with such representations. In Cognitive Science, indeed, different theories have been developed about how humans organize, reason, and retrieve conceptual information. The oldest one, known as "classical" or Aristotelian theory, states that concepts – the building blocks of our knowledge infrastructure – can be simply represented in terms of sets of necessary and sufficient conditions (and this is completely true, for instance, in mathematical concepts: e.g., an EQUILATERAL TRIANGLE can be classically defined as a regular polygon with three corners and three sides). In the mid-1970s, however, the previously mentioned experimental results from Rosch demonstrated its inadequacy for ordinary – or commonsense – concepts, which cannot be described in terms of necessary and sufficient traits. In particular, Rosch's results indicated that conceptual knowledge is organized in our minds in terms of prototypes. Since then, different theories of concepts have been proposed to explain different representational and reasoning aspects concerning the typicality or, in other terms, the commonsense effect. The most important one, in addition to the prototype theory, is the so-called "exemplar theory".[8]

Prototype and exemplar approaches, however, present significant differences. Prototype theory posits that knowledge about categories is stored in terms of some representation of the best instances in the category. For example, the concept "BIRD" should coincide with a representation of a prototypical bird (e.g., a robin). In the simpler versions of this approach, prototypes are represented

---

8 For the sake of completeness, it is worth noting that there is another theory that tries to explain the typicality effects phenomena, known as the "theory-theory" (Murphy, 2002). It adopts some form of a holistic point of view about concepts. According to some versions of theory-theories, concepts are analogous to theoretical terms in a scientific theory. For example, the concept "BIRD" is individuated by the role it plays in our mental theory of zoology. In other version of the approach, concepts themselves are identified with micro-theories of some sort. For example, the concept "BIRD" should be identified with a mentally represented micro-theory about birds. With respect to the prototypes and exemplars theories, however, which rely on more robust empirical data, the "theory-theory" approach is highly underspecified and more vaguely defined. As a consequence, at present, its theoretical and computational treatment is more problematic and not considered here.

as (possibly weighted) lists of features. This kind of representational assumption is strictly coupled with a specific categorization procedure known as prototypical reasoning. An example of such a reasoning strategy is the following – let us assume that we have to categorize a stimulus with the following features: "it has fur, it woofs, and it wags its tail". The result of a prototype-based categorization would be "dog", since these cues are associated with the prototype of dog. According to the exemplar view, on the other hand, a given category is mentally represented as a set of specific exemplars explicitly stored in memory: the mental representation of the concept "BIRD" is the set of the representations of (some of) the birds we have encountered during our lifetime. Also, the exemplars-based representational assumption is coupled with a specific categorization procedure. In particular, this theory posits that when we have to categorize a given stimulus, the similarity comparison is done not with "prototypes" but with the exemplars-representations that are available in our memory. For example: if an exemplar corresponding to the stimulus being categorized is available in our long-term memory, it is acknowledged that humans classify the stimulus by evaluating its similarity with regard to the exemplar, rather than with regard to the prototype associated with the underlying concepts. For example, a penguin is rather dissimilar from the prototype of a bird. However, if we already know an exemplar of penguin, and if we know that it is an instance of bird, it is easier for us to classify a new penguin as a bird with regard to a categorization process based on the similarity to the prototype of that category. This type of commonsense categorization is known in literature as "exemplars-based categorization" (and in this case the exemplar is favoured with regard to the prototype because of the phenomenon known as *old-item effect*).

As these examples show, prototype and exemplars-based theories make different assumptions about both the type of representations involved in categorization and the corresponding reasoning procedures leading to a given output. In particular, prototype models intend to capture only some central, and cognitively founded, aspects of the features of a concept, while the exemplars models represent *in toto* the particular knowledge of a certain entity. Concerning the categorization process, on the other hand, the decision of whether a target belongs to some category depends, for both prototype-based and exemplars-based cases, on the result of a similarity comparison computed between prototypical or exemplars representations and target representations. Despite this common mechanism, however, in the prototype view the computation of similarity is usually assumed to be *linear* (a property that is shared by the target and the prototype increases the similarity between both, independently of whether other properties are shared by them) while, according to the exemplar view, it is assumed to be *non-linear* (a property that is shared by the target and the exemplar is considered relevant only if there are also other shared properties between the two representations). An additional difference among the two approaches concerns the different assumptions about how such representations are stored in memory. According to prototype theorists, we store in our long-term memory only some parameters that characterize the categories we represent. According to exemplar theorists, we form memories of many encountered category members and we use, by default, these memories in cognitive tasks. This difference impacts the memory costs as well. In fact, prototypes are more synthetic representations, and occupy less memory space, compared to exemplars. On the other hand, the process of creation of a prototype requires more time and cognitive effort, while the mere storage of knowledge about exemplars is more parsimonious and less consuming because no abstraction is needed. Table 4.2 shows a synthetic comparison of these two representational and reasoning models. Interestingly enough, although these approaches have been largely considered competing ones, several results suggest that human subjects may use, on different occasions, different representations to categorize concepts. In particular, the first psychological study supporting the idea of multi-process theory was done by Malt (1989). Her study aimed at investigating whether people categorize and learn categories according to exemplar approaches or prototype-based models and she used behavioural measures such as categorization probability and reaction time. Her results demonstrate that not all subjects retrieve exemplars to categorize. Some use exemplars, a few rely on prototypes, and others appeal to both exemplars and prototypes. A protocol analysis of subjects' description of their categorization strategy confirms this interpretation. Malt writes (1989: 546–547):

> Three said they used only general features if the category in classifying the new exemplars. Nine said they used only similarity to old exemplars, and eight said that they used a mixture of category features and similarity to old exemplars. If reports accurately reflect the strategies used, then the data are composed of responses involving several different decision processes.

TABLE 4.2 Prototype models vs exemplar models

	Prototype models	*Exemplar models*
Memory storage	The prototype of each category is a sort of "average" description of all the exemplars experienced.	Many exemplars encountered are stored along with the category to which it belongs.
Memory costs	Not expensive. Prototypes are "synthetic" representations.	Expensive: the information concerning whole particular exemplars is stored.
Cognitive efforts	It is expensive to build the prototype. More time is requested.	It is parsimonious to use the exemplars knowledge.
Decision rule for categorization	Linear.	Not linear.
Inferential prediction	Not so good because it does not keep in memory all the traits.	Better in support predictions based on partial information.
Categorization effects	Similarity degree based on typicality.	Old items advantage effect.

This finding suggests that people can use either prototypes or exemplars in categorization tasks, which is consistent with other well-known studies such as those by Smith et al. (1997) and Smith and Minda (1998), the latter of which had experiments carried out with artificial stimuli. Smith et al. (1997), in fact, found that the performances of half the subjects of their experiments were best fit by a prototype model, while the performances of the other half were best fit by an exemplar model. This suggests that people can learn at least two different types of concepts – prototypes and exemplars – and that they can follow at least two strategies of categorization. Smith and Minda (1998) replicated these findings. Additionally, they found that during the learning phase, subjects' performances were best fitted by different models, suggesting that, when they learn to categorize artificial stimuli, subjects can switch from a strategy involving prototypes to a strategy involving exemplars. They also found that the learning path is influenced by the properties of the categories that subjects are presented with. For example, they show that categories with few, dissimilar members promoted the use of exemplar-based categorization strategies. Thus, psychological evidence suggests that we have at least two different mechanisms for categorizing. These mechanisms rely on different types of knowledge: prototypes and exemplars.

Such experimental evidence has led to the development of the so-called "heterogeneous hypothesis" about the nature of concepts. It hypothesizes that different types of conceptual representations exist (and may co-exist): prototypes, exemplars, classical representations, and so on (Lieto, 2014). All such representations, in this view, constitute different bodies of knowledge and contain different types of information associated with the same conceptual entity. Furthermore, each body of conceptual knowledge is distinguished by specific processes in which such representations are involved (e.g., in cognitive tasks like recognition, learning, categorization, etc.). In particular, prototypes and exemplars representations are associated with the possibility of dealing with typicality effects and non-monotonic strategies of reasoning and categorization, while classical representations (i.e., those based on necessary and/or sufficient conditions) are associated with a standard deductive mechanism of reasoning. Our human categorization capacity, therefore, is a direct consequence of having a heterogeneous set of representations for the same concepts and heterogeneous and integrated categorization strategies relying on prototypes, exemplars, and classical rule-based categorization (the latter one concerning the classical representations relying on necessary and sufficient conditions).

In the representational level of cognitive architectures, however, this *heterogeneity* is almost neglected. In general, despite the fact that some efforts have been made to implicitly address the presented problems, they are, as we will show next, not completely satisfactory for jointly solving both the mentioned limitations.

Knowledge size and knowledge heterogeneity in SOAR and ACT-R

After the above general clarification about the size and the (lack of) heterogeneity in the type of representations and the corresponding categorization procedures in cognitive architectures, let us see how and whether the SOAR and ACT-R models are compliant with their crucial requirements. In regards to SOAR, this symbolic architecture encounters the standard problems affecting symbolic formalisms at the representational level: it is not well equipped to deal with commonsense knowledge representation and reasoning (since approximate comparisons are hard and computationally intensive to implement with graph-like representations), and, as a consequence, the typology of encoded knowledge is biased towards the "classical" (but unsatisfactory) representation of concepts in terms of necessary and sufficient conditions. This characterization, however, is problematic for modelling real world concepts and, on the other hand, the so called commonsense knowledge components (i.e., those that allow the characterization and processing of conceptual information in terms of *typicality* and involving prototypical and exemplar-based representations and reasoning mechanisms) are absent. This problem arises despite the fact that the chunks in SOAR can be represented as sort of frame-like structures containing some commonsense (e.g., prototypical) information (Lieto, 2017). In fact, the main problem of this architecture with regard to the heterogeneity assumption relies on the fact that it does not specify how the prototypical knowledge components of a concept, and the corresponding commonsense reasoning strategies, can be integrated with exemplars and rule-based concepts and categorization strategies. With regard to the size problem, the SOAR knowledge level is also problematic. Indeed, despite some attempts to extend, in an efficient way, the Semantic Memory of the architecture with external lexical resources such as Wordnet[9] (Derbinsky, Laird, and Smith, 2010), SOAR agents are not endowed with general knowledge and can only process ad-hoc built (or task-specific learned) symbolic knowledge structures. Also in the case of the above-mentioned extension, it is worth noticing that WordNet is not a knowledge base but a lexical database.

In contrast to SOAR, ACT-R allows the representation of information in terms of prototypes and exemplars and the performance, selectively, of either prototype or exemplar-based categorization. This means that this architecture allows the modeller to manually specify which kind of categorization strategy to employ according to his specific needs. Such an architecture, however, only partially addresses the homogeneity problem, since it does not allow to represent, jointly, these different types of commonsense representations for the same conceptual entity (i.e., it does not assume a heterogeneous perspective). As a consequence, it is also not able to autonomously decide which of the corresponding reasoning procedures to activate (e.g., prototypes or exemplars) nor is it able to provide a framework able to manage the interaction of such different reasoning

---

9 WordNet is a widely known lexical database for the English language, developed at Princeton University (Miller, 1995). Rather than organizing terms alphabetically (like ordinary dictionaries, where senses are possibly scattered) WN groups terms into synonyms sets called "synsets", which are equipped with short definitions and usage examples. Such sets are represented as the nodes of a large semantic network, where the intervening edges represent a number of semantic relations among synset elements (such as hyponymy, hypernymy, antonymy, meronymy, holonymy, etc.).

strategies (however, it is worth noticing that its overall architectural environment provides, at least in principle, the possibility of implementing cascade reasoning processes triggering one another). Even if, in such architecture, some attempts exist concerning the design of harmonization strategies between different types of commonsense conceptual categorizations (e.g., there is a famous exemplars- and rule-based computational model, developed by Anderson and Betz, 2001), they do not handle the problem concerning the interaction of the prototype- or exemplars-based processes according to the results coming from experimental cognitive science. For example, the well-known phenomenon *"old item effect"*, privileging exemplars with regard to prototypes, is not modelled.

Concerning the "size" criterion, the model developed by Salvucci et al. (2014) extended the knowledge model of the Declarative Memory of ACT-R with a world-level knowledge base such as DBpedia (i.e., the semantic version of Wikipedia, represented in a machine-readable semantic format); and a previous one in Ball, Rodgers, and Gluck (2004) proposed an integration of the ACT-R Declarative and Procedural Memory with the Cyc ontology (one of the widest knowledge bases currently available, containing more than 230,000 concepts, see Lenat, 1995). Both wide-coverage integrated semantic resources, however, represent conceptual information in terms of symbolic structures and encounter the standard problems that affect this class of formalisms, also discussed above in the case of SOAR; i.e., they assume the representation of conceptual information in "classical" terms and not, let us say, in prototypical or exemplars-based terms. In addition, since these extended representations are not commonsense based, it is not possible to perform either prototype- or exemplars-based categorization, nor to eventually integrate two such different types or commonsense processes that are ubiquitous in human cognition.

Summing up, with regard to the knowledge homogeneity problem, the components needed to fully reconcile the heterogeneity approach with ACT-R are present from a representational point of view, however, they are not integrated. Regarding the size problem, as with SOAR, ACT-R agents are usually equipped with task-specific knowledge and not with general cross-domain knowledge.[10]

In light of the arguments presented above, it can be argued, therefore, that the current proposed solutions for dealing with the knowledge problems in cognitive architectures are not completely satisfactory. In particular, the integrations with huge world-level ontological knowledge bases can be considered a necessary solution for solving the size problem. It is, however, insufficient for dealing with the knowledge homogeneity problem and with the integration of the common-sense conceptual mechanisms activated on heterogeneous bodies of knowledge, as is assumed in the heterogeneous representational perspective. In the next section, we outline an alternative solution that has been proposed to account for both for the heterogeneous aspects in conceptualization and the size problem.

---

10 For a much more fine-grained and extended analysis on these aspects we recommend Lieto, Lebiere, and Oltramari (2018), wherein the SPAUN model (Eliasmith, 2012; Blouw, 2016) is additionally analyzed on the same dimensions.

DUAL PECCS

DUAL PECCS is a cognitively inspired categorization system that I have developed over the last few years at the University of Turin, in collaboration with my colleagues Daniele P. Radicioni and Valentina Rho. The acronym stands for **DUAL** **P**rototypes and **E**xemplars **C**onceptual **C**ategorization **S**ystem and suggests that this system explicitly assumes the heterogeneous representational hypothesis. In particular, DUAL PECCS explicitly implements the following cognitive assumptions: (i) the fact that conceptual representations are heterogeneous co-referring representational structures delegated to different computational frameworks and (ii) the fact that the different reasoning strategies executed on such representations are harmonized according to the dual process theory of reasoning and rationality (for the details see Lieto, 2014, 2019). In addition, the representational level of DUAL PECCS (and the corresponding knowledge processing mechanisms) has been successfully integrated with the representational counterpart of the ACT-R and SOAR cognitive architectures by extending, *de facto*, the knowledge representation and processing capabilities of such cognitive architectures that are based on diverse representational assumptions.

Let us explore, in some more detail, this system: the heterogeneous conceptual architecture of DUAL PECCS includes "typical" commonsense representations (i.e., prototypes and exemplars) and a "classical" representation. All these different bodies of knowledge point to the same conceptual entity and are connected via Wordnet (the procedures for the anchoring for these different types of representations are described in Lieto, Radicioni, and Rho, 2017). An example of the heterogeneous conceptual architecture of DUAL PECCS is provided in Figure 4.3. The figure shows how it represents the concept "TIGER". In this case, the prototypical representation grasps information such as tigers are usually conceptualized as felines with yellow fur and stripes, typically with a tail, etc.; the exemplar-based representations grasp information on individuals. For example, it may represent an individual Siberian tiger, with white fur.

Within the system, both these types of typicality-based representations are made available by using the framework of the conceptual spaces proposed by Gärdenfors (2000). Conceptual spaces (CSs) can be thought of as a particular class of vectorial representations[11] where knowledge is represented as a set of two features with which is associated a geometrical (topological or metrical) structure. Such a framework allows the adoption of standard similarity metrics to determine the distance between instances and concepts within the space. In such a framework, the conceptual features can be directly related to perceptual mechanisms; examples of this are temperature, weight, brightness, pitch, etc. In other cases, they can be

---

11 In this class of representations, the idea is that concepts are represented as vectors of features. Recently, this class of representations has been widely used in a particular area of Computational Linguistics known as Distributional Semantics (Mikolov et al., 2013; Pennington, Socher, and Manning, 2014).

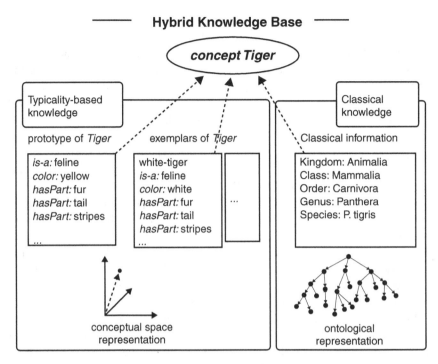

FIGURE 4.3   An example of the hybrid conceptual architecture in DUAL PECCS.

more abstract in nature. This framework was selected since it allows the modelling of prototypes and exemplars in a straightforward way. In this setting, indeed, concepts correspond to convex regions, and regions with different geometrical properties correspond to different sorts of concepts. Here, prototypes and prototypical reasoning have a natural geometrical interpretation: prototypes correspond to the geometrical centre of a convex region (the centroid). Also exemplars can be represented as points in a multidimensional space, and their similarity can be computed as the intervening distance between each of the two points, based on some suitable metric (such as Euclidean and Manhattan distance, etc.).

On the other hand, in DUAL PECCS, the representation of "classical" information (e.g., facts like Tiger ⊑ Mammalia, etc.; that is to say, "tigers are also mammals") is represented by a class of symbolic formalism that are nowadays called "ontologies" and illustrates a sort of new type of semantic network. More specifically, the "classical" component of DUAL PECCS is equipped with the Cyc ontology (Lenat, 1995), which, as mentioned, is one of the widest knowledge bases currently available, containing more than 230,000 concepts.

From a reasoning perspective, one of the main novelties introduced by DUAL PECCS consists of the fact that it is explicitly designed according to the flow of interaction between commonsense categorization processes (based on prototypes and exemplars and operating on conceptual spaces representations) and the standard rule-based deductive processes (operating on the ontological conceptual component). The harmonization regarding such different classes of mechanisms has been devised based on tenets from the dual process theory of reasoning, postulated by Daniel Kahneman, which assumes two different types of processes (System 1 processes and System 2 processes) that are distinguished, among the other things, by the fact System 1 processes execute approximate reasoning in a fast way, while System 2 processes are assumed to be slower and more logical and deliberative in nature (Kahneman, 2011). In DUAL PECCS, the Type 1 processes are associated to with commonsense representation and concerns the exemplars- and prototypes-based categorization, while the Type 2 processes are associated with the symbolic representational component executing standard deductive categorization. Interestingly, in DUAL PECCS the interaction of the categorization processes occurring *within* the System 1 (i.e., prototypes- and exemplars-based categorization) has been devised and is dealt with within the CSs component. Such a framework, indeed, has proven to provide a natural way to model both prototypes and exemplars representations and their corresponding reasoning processes (including their interaction). In this way, DUAL PECCS is able to satisfy the heterogeneity requirement for both the represented knowledge and the integrated reasoning mechanisms executed on different bodies of knowledge.

In regards to the size problem, finally, the grounding of the CSs representational component with symbolic structures has enabled the integration with wide-coverage knowledge bases such as Cyc. Thus, the solution adopted in DUAL PECCS is able to deal with both the size and the knowledge homogeneity problems affecting cognitive architectures. In particular, the extension of the Declarative Memories of the current cognitive architectures with this external cognitive system allowed to empower the knowledge processing and categorization capabilities of such general architectures (and an important role, in this respect, is played by the CSs component). Despite the fact that there is still room for improvements and further investigation, this seems a promising way to deal with both knowledge problems discussed in this paper. In addition to these theoretical supportive arguments, however, DUAL PECCS has also been empirically tested in a conceptual categorization task of commonsense linguistic descriptions similar to riddles (i.e., of the form: "What is the big feline with yellow fur and black stripes?" etc.). This kind of task is a very difficult one from an AI perspective since, in commonsense reasoning, state-of-the-art AI systems like IBM's Watson obtain very poor results (see Davis and Marcus, 2015). In addition, the types of linguistic stimuli to categorize were developed by a multidisciplinary team composed of psychologists, linguists, and philosopher following the dictates of the well-known psychological test known as "Word Reasoning", consisting of identifying a concept based on one to three clues (see Ohlsson et al., 2012). The results obtained by DUAL PECCS are promising, both when compared to human performances (with an overlapping of 89% of the responses, see Lieto, Radicioni, and Rho, 2017, for the results in detail) and compared to other artificial systems like Google, Bing, or Wolphram Alpha (see Lieto et al., 2017, for a detailed analysis of the obtained results). An additional advantage of the proposed approach lies in the fact that it limits the computational complexity of the commonsense reasoning strategy to linear time, since the mechanism of typicality-based categorization technically corresponds to measuring the semantic relatedness of an input "query vector" (in which the linguistic input is transformed) with respect to a vectoral knowledge-base of conceptual spaces (and this process can be solved in linear time with respect to the size of the knowledge base). As a consequence, this case study seems to suggest that a cognitive design approach in the modern AI is also an important aspect to consider in order to progress toward more human-like and human-level AI systems.

Summing up, the DUAL PECCS categorization system, integrated with ACT-R and SOAR cognitive architectures, is able to structurally model both problematic issues mentioned in the previous sections of this chapter. But how is this difference reflected if we use the "Minimal Cognitive Grid"? If we consider the functional/structural ratio we have seen – for the conceptual categorization process – that DUAL PECCS has a lower ratio (and therefore a better structural accuracy) with respect to both the categorization models of ACT-R and SOAR, aiming at dealing with the size and the heterogeneity problems. While both architectures have provided models to extend the size of their knowledge base, indeed, no one has been able to integrate prototypes- and exemplars-based representations and reasoning the way DUAL PECCS has. For the "generality" criterion, there is a double discourse to make: if we consider "generality" for the task of categorization, then DUAL PECCS is evidently able to model the diverse spectrum of the categorization capacities exhibited by humans (i.e., exemplars-, prototypes-, and rule-based categorization) and, as such, is more general than the other computational models of categorization available in ACT-R and SOAR. In addition, if we consider that the DUAL PECCS categorization system is actually integrated with ACT-R and SOAR, then this system itself also becomes "general" since it can be considered an extension of two candidates of Unified Theories of Cognition. The system is not general, however, if we consider the use of its architecture in other tasks[12] and this consideration also holds for the other ACT-R and SOAR extended categorization models. In regards to the performance match, finally, the DUAL PECCS system is, to the best of my knowledge, the only one currently implementing – in an integrated and cognitively compliant way – prototype-, exemplars-, and rule-based categorization. Therefore, it cannot be compared with the other computational models extending the declarative memories of ACT-R and SOAR. Concerning, however, its comparison with human responses, it is interesting not only for the above-mentioned convergence

12 As I reported in a recent podcast interview for the programme *Scientific Sense* (available here podcast.scientificsense.net/824 on different platforms), the possibility of using Imagenet, instead of Wordnet, as a grounding element for connecting the different types of representation is currently under investigation. Should this attempt prove to be feasible, we could use the same architecture for both visual and language categorization. Currently, however, there are no results to report on this attempt.

on human-level performances for such a difficult task but also for the "execution time". As mentioned, in fact, the computational complexity of the adopted commonsense reasoning strategy in the CSs framework is linear with respect to the size of the vectoral knowledge base, and this represents a great advantage with respect, for example, to the non-monotonic extensions of logical formalisms, which are often intractable. As a consequence, the response times of the system for the "fast" categorization procedure were produced within a second or less. Finally, in regards to the analysis of the errors, we noticed that the vast majority of errors of the system were due to confusion between exemplars and prototypes; in particular, in 21% of the considered stimuli, an exemplar representation was returned by the system in spite of the expected prototype (representing the response provided by humans for the same stimulus). This error was caused by the fact that DUAL PECCS implements the above-mentioned *old item effect*, i.e., if exemplar-based representations in the KB are equipped with typical information closely matching the linguistic description being categorized, then such representations are always favoured with respect to their prototypical counterparts. However, this fact, although in line with psychological experimental evidence where exemplars – if available and similar enough to the stimulus to categorize – are mostly returned as the first choice, resulted in being counterintuitive for very general descriptions situated at a high level of abstraction. For example, given the input description, "What animal eats bananas?', DUAL PECCS retrieved the representation of the exemplar associated with "roloway_monkey", while the expected output, based on the answers provided by human subjects, is the generic prototype of "monkey" since the provided description is quite general. As we noted in the paper presenting DUAL PECCS, this result is interesting since our cognitively inspired system suggests that something in the theory derived by the experimental results needs revision. As we pointed out,

> This particular class of errors deserves additional clarification in future works: albeit emerged experimenting the computational model, it also suggests that additional analysis is needed in the theoretical debate about exemplars and prototypes. Our results seem to demand deepening the heuristics that steer our categorical choices when the stimulus at hand spans different levels of abstraction. Therefore also from an epistemological perspective this result is interesting, since it shows how cognitively-inspired computational models of cognition taking into account a structuralist perspective, can fruitfully provide insights to the theoretical counterparts that they implement, in a continuous cycle of interaction between theoretical and experimental settings.
>
> *(Lieto, Radicioni, and Rho, 2017: 32)*

This kind of result is exactly the type we look for in the context of a computationally grounded science of the mind.

5

EVALUATING THE PERFORMANCES OF ARTIFICIAL SYSTEMS

Abstract

This chapter introduces the main proposals that have been developed in order to evaluate the performance of artificial systems (cognitively inspired or not) and to justify the ascription of faculties from the "cognitive" vocabulary (like "intelligence") to such systems. After introducing the Turing Test, its problematic aspects, and some of the main modifications proposed (e.g., the Super Turing Test and other variations), we will analyze other frameworks like the Newell Test for a theory of cognition and other tasks and challenges that have been used – with different purposes – as a testbed for the evaluation of artificial systems. These tasks range from the RoboCup World Soccer to the DARPA Challenges for autonomous vehicles to the recently proposed Winograd Schema Challenge and the RoboCup@Home. We will analyze these proposals both in light of their eventual explanatory role in the context of a computationally driven science of the mind and with respect to their actual capacity for evaluating the "intelligence" of artificial systems.

"Thinking" machines and Turing Test(s)

Determining to what extent an artificial system can be defined as "intelligent" as humans (or other animals) has been a problematic aspect since the beginning of the early research on intelligent machines. Usually the arguments used in support of the idea that machines can be intelligent follow this schema – premise 1: an entity is intelligent if shows a given behaviour X; premise 2: it is possible to build artificial systems (both embodied and not) that are able to manifest the behaviour X; conclusion: the machines able to exhibit that manifest behaviour can be claimed to be "intelligent". This argument has been subjected to different objections. The first one, called the "*behaviouristic objection*", concerns the fact that the first premise is questionable – an artificial system able to display a certain behaviour does not necessarily imply any understanding or intelligence about the actions or tasks that it is able to perform. A second objection, which we could call "*technological pessimism*", frames as questionable the second premise: in this case there are doubts about the possibility of an artificial system actually being programmed to exhibit a target behaviour that is externally described as an "intelligent" one. In the following sections, these objections, along with others, will be overviewed by exploring some of the main proposals concerning the evaluation of artificial systems able to exhibit intelligent behaviour.

The first, in this line, was the proposal from Alan Turing in his famous paper "Computing machinery and intelligence" (Turing, 1950). The British mathematician and inventor of the abstract computing machine bearing his name suggested that, in order to determine what answer to provide to the question, "Can machines think?" it was possible to use a sort of "indirect" test, called the "Turing Test" (TT) or "Imitation game" (an overview of this topic is provided in Epstein, Roberts, and Beber, 2009). In this game three "players" are involved: two human beings (one working as an "interrogator" and the other being asked to provide the answer) and a computing machine, which also has the role of answering the questions posed by the human interrogator. Within this "game" the interrogator is assumed to be in a sort of "blind" situation: i.e., s/he does not see who/what (the computing machine or the other human being) is responding to the questions s/he is asking. Indeed, s/he is supposed to communicate with them only indirectly (e.g., through a video display and keyboard) by asking them questions and reading their answers.

The goal of the game, for the interrogator, is to discover as quickly as possible which is the human and which is the machine. To achieve this goal, the interrogator can ask any question. In this way, the human player is assumed to behave in a way that would help the interrogator, while the machine is programmed to deceive the interrogator for as long as possible. According to Turing, indeed, the more the machine is able to resist and deceive the human interrogator, the more this can been seen as an indirect hint of its "intellectual" ability (a pictorial representation of the situation hypothesized in the TT is available in the Figure 5.1). Here is an interrogator/machine conversation imagined by Turing in his paper:

INTERROGATOR: In the first line of your sonnet which reads, "Shall I compare three to a summer's day", would not "a spring day" do as well or better?
COMPUTER: I wouldn't scan.
INTERROGATOR: How about "a winter's day?" That would scan all right.
COMPUTER: Yes, but nobody wants to be compared to a winter's day.
INTERROGATOR: Would you say Mr. Pickwick reminded you of Christmas?
COMPUTER: In a way.
INTERROGATOR: Yet Christmas is a winter's day, and I do not think Mr. Pickwick would mind the comparison.
COMPUTER: I don't think you are serious. By a winter's day one means a typical winter's day, rather than a special one like Christmas

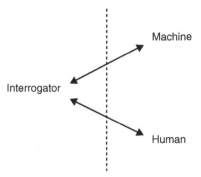

FIGURE 5.1 A pictorial representation of the "Imitation game".

As pointed out by Levesque (2017) in his recent book, we are today still far from building systems capable of this level of conversation. Turing's point, however, was to investigate if – assuming that we could build such a system – we could ascribe, from the vocabulary of folk psychology, terms like "understanding", "thinking", and "intelligence" to such machines.

As mentioned, Turing assumed that the machine, in order to obtain a more realistic effect in playing the Imitation game, is allowed to "cheat", by occasionally making mistakes. For example, he explicitly wrote:

> It is claimed that the interrogator could distinguish the machine from the human simply by setting them a number of problems in arithmetic. The machine would be unmasked because of its deadly accuracy. The reply to this is simple. The machine (programmed to play the game) would not attempt to give the right answers to the arithmetic problems. It would deliberately introduce mistakes in a manner calculated to confuse the interrogator.
>
> *(Turing, 1950: 448)*

Similar cheating strategies were used also by the ELIZA chat-bot program, mentioned in the Chapter 1 (footnote 14), developed by Joseph Weizenbaum in 1966, which attempted to mimic the dialogue capabilities of a psychotherapist by employing a number of simple strategies like (1) the use of keywords and pre-canned responses (for instance, answering, "Can you tell me more about your family?" when the human wrote, "Perhaps I could learn to get along with my mother..."); (2) by parroting the human interrogator (e.g., if the human wrote, "My girlfriend made me come here", the system would have rebutted, "Your boyfriend made you come here?"); or (3) by asking very general questions (e.g., "In what way?" or "Can you give a specific example?"). Despite these simple strategies, it is interesting that humans were quick to attribute human-level intelligence to such a simple program. In this respect, experiments with ELIZA can be viewed as the first attempts to deal with the TT. As a consequence they also pointed out some of its limitations.

The TT, in fact, has been interpreted in a number of different ways: as a way to provide a general definition of thought, or intelligence; as an operational criterion for ascribing intelligence to artificial systems; or as a test for determining the adequacy of simulative models of cognition. As mentioned, for such diverse interpretations there are corresponding different critiques. The most important one concerns the behaviouristic objection mentioned before. In particular, this test has been criticized because it only refers to the manifest behaviour of a given system and no claim can be made about the internal mechanisms that have led to that behaviour. This makes the test an insufficient criterion for the empirical validation of a simulative model (see e.g., Cordeschi, 2002). Another well-known criticism, developed in the copious literature on this theme, concerns its excessive anthropocentrism. The TT, indeed, explicitly targets human and human-like "thinking" and, therefore, cannot be used to provide a universal criterion for attributing intelligence (this is also called the "*chauvinistic objection*"). Concerning this aspect, Turing himself clarified that he did not intend to propose the test as a way to define "intelligence" in a general sense. In his paper, Turing readily acknowledges that one could have a situation where intelligent beings are able (or not able) to pass the test simply by not having human-like intellect:

> May not machines carry out something which ought to be described as thinking but which is very different from what a man does? This objection is a very strong one, but at least we can say that if, nevertheless, a machine can be constructed to play the imitation game satisfactorily, we need not be troubled by this objection.

Another well-known and strong objection raised towards the TT concerns the fact that it is only limited to the linguistic behaviour (i.e., it is only a "language-based" experiment, while all the other cognitive faculties are not tested). This drawback has also downsized the role of the proposed test as a "general test for human intelligence" since, as the psychologist Howard Gardner pointed out in his "multiple intelligence theory", there are different kinds of modality-specific "intelligent abilities" concerning human beings. And verbal-linguistic abilities are only one of those (Gardner, 2011). Another problem, finally, concerns the subjective evaluation of the interrogator. Different human interrogators, indeed, could judge in a different way the same machine behaviour. Such criticisms, however, may be considered as not all having the same weight. As noticed in Frixione (2015), for example, while the chauvinistic objection can be considered less problematic when the TT is used within an empirical study of the (human) mind, the other ones – concerning the "linguistic", the "behaviouristic", and the "subjectivistic" bias – are much more serious. Given this state of affairs, in fact, different, modified versions of the TT have been proposed. For example, Stevan Harnad (Harnad, 2001) proposed the so-called Total Turing Test (TTT), a version of the TT extended to take into account any kind of input and output and that, consequently, assumes to have a robotic system, with perceptors and actuators, as a "machine". Such a proposal, however, while allows one to deal with the "linguistic objection", does not make any progress on the subjectivistic and overall behaviouristic objection. The latter, in particular, still holds, since nothing can be said about the compliance (if any) of the computational mechanisms used by such an embodied system to determine its – eventually intelligent – behaviour (described as such by an external observer). This fact, as a consequence, affects the use of this variant of the TT as a "general" test for intelligence. In addition, passing the TTT per se cannot be considered a sufficient condition for validating a simulative model of some cognitive phenomena, since – as with the TT – the TTT does not allow the explanation of any mental processing activity. This point has been stressed, for example, by Pylyshyn (1984), Newell and Simon, and Philipp Johnson-Laird; on this, see Roberto Cordeschi (2002). In the context of a computational cognitive account of the sciences of the mind, alternative suggestions have been made to use the TT in such a way that the interrogator could unmask the machine and its eventual non-compliance with "human-like" thinking and intelligence. It has been proposed, for example, to "test" the artificial system by proposing it solve behavioural tests for which there are already established results in psychological literature. For example: the interrogator, in order to unmask the machine, could take advantage of her/his empirical knowledge about certain behaviour regularities and could find a way to use, in both the TT and TTT version, her/his knowledge about, for example, the *"semantic priming"* effect[1] (as proposed by French 1990) or the *conjunction fallacy* (see footnote 3 in Chapter 3) or other well-known heuristics. This would allow her/him to see whether the artificial system replies in way that is similar to a human's response and if it respects other behavioural parameters (e.g., response times). As reported in Frixione (2015), this possibility was considered by Robert French (1990) as a flaw of the test (at least with respect to its interpretation as a "general" test for the attribution of intelligence to an artificial system) since, in this way, it could have been easier for the interrogator to discover if his/her interlocutor is a man or a machine. This critique has been rejected by scholars like Copeland (2000), who specifies how, according to the original dictate of Turing, this kind of test would be illegitimate since "the specifications of the TT are clear: the interrogator is allowed only to put questions (535)". As a response to Copeland, however, one could easily argue that the testing of such "behavioural regularities" could be easily put in forms of questions during a completely open conversation. Of course, in the case of the TTT, the constraint according to which the interrogator is only allowed to put forward questions no longer holds (since the communication is assumed to be also possible via other channels).

---

1 Semantic priming (McNamara, 2005) is a well-known psychological effect corresponding to the fact that, in word recognition tasks, during the presentation of pairs of semantically related words (e.g., "cat" and "dog"), the recognition of the second word of the pair ("dog" in this case) is always facilitated (or "primed") with respect to the presentation of semantically unrelated ones (e.g., as in the case of the pair, "cat" and "surf").

However, in such a case, it is not clear what instrument the interrogator could use to check the provided answers. Despite such limitations, the proposal made by French is *prima facie* interesting from a cognitive perspective since it presupposes that, if a system is able to match human performance in dealing with these kinds of problems, it could deceive the interrogator by showing human-like compliance with respect to her/his expectations. Such "human-likeness" could be measured also by resorting to additional psychometric tests and evaluations. Upon a deeper analysis, however, despite the fact that a system able to pass the test in the described conditions should be one of those explicitly addressing stronger constraints imposed on its models, it is worth noting that this hypothetical human-like compliance in terms of "performance" would not necessarily imply that any underlying "structural" simulative model of cognition is actually running on the "machine" exhibiting that behaviour. As we saw in Chapter 3, indeed, the *"performance match"* is only one of the three criteria identified for ascribing an explanatory role to an artificial model. In addition, as Frixione points out (Frixione, 2015), even in this case, passing the TT or the TTT

> should not be sufficient to validate a simulative model of cognition because it ignores: (i) any form of non-behavioral empirical evidence (such as, for example, evidence coming from the neurosciences); (ii) other relevant "cognitive virtues", such as simplicity, consistency with other accepted theories, refusal of ad hoc solutions, and so on.
>
> *(132)*

From this point of view, then, the behaviouristic problem of the TT, in all of its forms, remains. Also in the case of a "Super-simplified" TT, having only an interrogator judging if a machine is intelligent in a non-blind configuration (i.e., the interrogator knows that s/he is interacting with a machine), would not be unproblematic. Here, indeed, the problem is that the mere knowledge that we are dealing with a machine will bias our judgment as to whether that machine can think or not, as we may bring certain preconceptions to the table (see De Melo and Terada, 2019). For example, some people/interrogators could have higher expectations of the machine (with respect to the human beings), and therefore their judgments could be influenced by the fact that they "raise the bar for intelligence", while others could be less demanding with the machines. The "blind" situation eliminates, in principle, this risk.

Overall, I have indicated a selection, relevant for our purposes, of some problematic accounts raised towards the TT and its variations.[2] In particular, I have pointed out how the TT and the TTT cannot be considered suitable tests for a simulative model or cognition nor as "general" test for intelligence due

---

2 The list, however, is far from being complete. For a more detailed account, we recommend again Epstein, Roberts, and Beber (2009), and for a critique of many allegations against the TT we refer, instead, to LaCurts (2011).

to their intrinsic anthropocentrism. Such tests can only provide an account of human-level performances in specific or integrated tasks, respectively (with the only exceptions of the TT in its variation with behavioural experiments that, in principle, can offer other also some hints to evaluate the human-like compliance of the obtained performances). As mentioned, one of the major weaknesses of such tests is the fact that they are biased by a subjective evaluation procedure.

In the following part, we will introduce another influential critique of the TT (extendible to all its variants), proposed by the philosopher John Searle in his famous Chinese Room experiment. The experiment shows how such tests, being behavioural in nature, cannot be used for attributing an intrinsic "intelligence" (in the "human sense") to the systems that eventually pass them. Nonetheless, they can be used for a superficial evaluation of their "performances" with respect to human performances: i.e., they could be useful to test their human-level capacities.

The Chinese Room

The Chinese Room is a though experiment proposed by John Searle as a critique of the behaviouristic and functional account proposed by the TT. Searle (1999) describes the Chinese Room experiment as follows:

> Imagine a native English speaker who knows no Chinese locked in a room full of boxes of Chinese symbols (a data base) together with a book of instructions for manipulating the symbols (the program). Imagine that people outside the room send in other Chinese symbols which, unknown to the person in the room, are questions in Chinese (the input). And imagine that by following the instructions in the program the man in the room is able to pass out Chinese symbols which are correct answers to the questions (the output). The program enables the person in the room to pass the Turing Test for understanding Chinese but he does not understand a word of Chinese.

As this passage suggests, the "man in the room" manipulating unknown symbols according to a program (the book of instructions) is the equivalent of a machine. And, if a machine able to perform this task existed, it – just like the English-speaking human – will not understand anything, even though it provides the correct output. The core of Searle's critique is that the simple execution of a program manipulating symbols at the syntactic level (i.e., without understanding anything at the semantic one) does not constitute proof of the actual intelligence of the system manifesting that behaviour.[3] The obtained behaviour can, in fact,

---

3 It is worth noting that the Searle's critique is not only directed to the "symbolic approach" or the "Physical Symbol System Hypothesis" as a superficial analysis could suggest (of course, these were the main available approaches used in the AI of the 1980s). His critique, however,

only be considered the result of a simulation of intelligence. As a consequence of this state of affairs, it is improper to attribute to any computing machine any kind of "thinking" or "understanding" capacity. What is lacking in such machines, according to Searle, is indeed the intrinsic "intentionality" of performing the tasks. Only in that case could we say that a machine has a mind, is intelligent, etc. Such intentionality, however, is not grasped by an AI program performing the task. In fact, as in the case of the teleological explanation seen in Chapter 3, it is only externally "attributed" by the programmer (who decides the meaning of the symbols the program is going to manipulate) or by an external observer who adopts an "intentional stance" towards the observed behaviour of the system. On the basis of these considerations, Searle introduced the notorious distinction between "Strong AI" (i.e., the position assuming that computational models, embodied or not, can possess a "mind", a "consciousness", etc. in the same way as human beings)[4] and "Weak AI" (the position according to which computational models can simulate human behaviour and thinking but cannot pretend, as the Chinese Room argument shows, to possess any kind of "real" cognitive state).

Searle's argument has received both critiques and endorsements. I will not detail here all the different disputes and replies to the argument since they will drive us too far from the purposes of this book (a good, synthetic, overview is provided in the entry of the *Stanford Encyclopaedia of Philosophy* – https://plato.stanford.edu/entries/chinese-room/); it is important however, to point out that current AI and cognitive modelling research are perfectly aligned with the Weak AI hypothesis. This does not make weaker either of the disciplines: AI researchers, indeed, continue to build better systems with the purpose of them being useful for human beings and being able to, in principle, perform better than humans in specific tasks; computational cognitive scientists, on the other hand, continue to build "structural" computational simulations of cognitive processes without pretending to build any system able to really be described as "intelligent" or "conscious" in the proper human sense. This latter assumption is also the underlying one of this entire book and is in contrast to the popular (but incorrect) *vulgata* that see computational models of cognition as belonging to the class of systems espousing the "Strong AI" hypothesis and, as such, assuming that such models (of minds or brains) can actually be considered "minds" or "brains" in the very same way as human ones. As described hitherto: artificial models of minds/brains can simulate the human-like mechanisms that determine a given

---

applies to computational approaches in general. In fact, despite some attempts of connectionists posing counter-objections (e.g., Paul and Patricia Churchland, 1990), a neural AI system able to perform the same tasks described by Searle would still need to "manipulate" (by adjusting the weights in the net) a distributed pattern of representations that, at the highest levels of the network, would have a symbol-like function (and this abstractive capacity and functionality is exactly the target of deep learning; see Goodfellow et al., 2016).

4 Searle's exact formulation of the Strong AI hypothesis is: "the appropriately programmed computer really is a mind, in the sense that computers given the right programs can be literally said to understand and have other cognitive states" (Searle, 1980).

behaviour, and this can enable the understanding of some hidden mechanistic dynamics. This understanding can eventually be exported in the context of non-computational investigations (e.g., in psychology, biology, or neuroscience). Such artificial models of the mind, therefore, can be used to understand mental phenomena without pretending that that they are the real phenomena that they are modelling. Using a famous analogy proposed by Searle himself: just as a model of the weather is not the weather, a model of the human mind is not a human mind. As a consequence, and as stated repeatedly since the preface, artificial models of minds/brains can be seen as representative of mental/brain activities only to a certain degree, depending on their level of structural accuracy. And that's perfectly fine.

The Newell test for a theory of cognition

Newell (1980, 1990) proposed a set of criteria to evaluate to what extent an artificial system can be said to provide the computational background for a theory of cognition (or better a simulative account of such a theory). In a 2003 paper that appeared in *Behavioural and Brain Science*, John Anderson and Christian Lebiere (Anderson and Lebiere, 2003) distilled this list into 12 criteria that they called the "Newell Test for a Theory of Cognition". As the authors write, these criteria are functional constraints on the cognitive architecture. The first nine reflect things that the architecture must achieve to implement human intellectual capacity, and the last three reflect constraints on how these functions are to be achieved. As such, they do not reflect everything that one should ask of a cognitive theory.

The distilled criteria are the following ones:

1 *flexible behaviour*: i.e., for Newell, a system with a theory of cognition should be flexible enough to learn and perform almost arbitrary cognitive tasks with a high degree of expertise;

2 *real-time performance*: this criterion calls for systems able to solve the task in "human time", which Newell calls "real-time";

3 *adaptive behaviour*: cognitive architectures should have mechanisms that enable their adaptivity;

4 *vast knowledge base*: this criterion calls for the same necessity of the "*size*" requirement that was considered in the previous chapter for the analysis of the knowledge level in cognitive architectures. Having a system with huge knowledge base, indeed, immediately poses computational and cognitive problems concerning the retrieval of the correct knowledge, given a task to solve, that are neglected or hidden under the carpet when such systems employ only toy knowledge bases.

5 *Dynamic behaviour*: for Newell, a system with a theory of cognition must be able to deal with the unexpected and with a changing environment;

6 *knowledge integration*: different kinds of knowledge should be integrated in order to endow a cognitive architecture with the full range of inferential

capabilities that human beings are able to exhibit: induction, deduction, abduction, analogy, etc. This aspect partially overlaps with the "heterogeneity" criterion proposed in our previous analysis, since Newell assumed that all such inferences could have been tackled with different types of integrated "symbolic systems". On the other hand, the heterogeneity criterion calls for a heterogeneous approach for knowledge integration, coupling symbols with diverse representations and reasoning procedures.

7   *Natural language*: a cognitive architecture must be able to deal with natural language interaction;

8   *learning*: a cognitive architecture should be able to learn and acquire competences;

9   *consciousness*: a computational theory of cognition should possess a theory of consciousness and model it. This aspect is controversial since, for human beings as well, there is no consensus about a unifying theory of consciousness; nonetheless, many computational models trying to address this issue exist. As mentioned, the last three criteria correspond to different types of constraints through which the above-mentioned skills should develop:

10 *development*: the overall abilities described above should unfold and grow over time;

11 *evolution*: a cognitive architecture should reflect the evolutionary processes that have selected certain mechanisms and heuristics; and

12 *brain*: Newell suggests that the components of the cognitive architectures should be mapped onto brain structures and, in addition, that these matches should develop in a neural implementation such that the computation of the neural structures match the one of the assigned components. The latter criterion evidences how Newell, after an initial period of indifference towards neuroscience, started to consider the "biological band" an important aspect to enrich the constraints posed by its systems (in particular SOAR) at the highest bands.

These criteria, very similar in nature to some of the *desiderata* for the development of cognitive architectures presented in Chapter 3, were used to evaluate two different theories of cognition (i.e., ACT-R and classical connectionism) in a qualitative way. Given the type of defined criteria it was, indeed, impossible to make a stricter comparison. For most of the criteria, in fact, there is not a direct way to assess the extent to which a given computational cognitive theory can actually be compared or ranked with respect to them. In other words, such criteria have been called "general", since they cover all the major aspects of the cognitive spectrum, but in most cases they are generic (i.e., highly underspecified) and, as such, affected by subjective judgements. As Anderson and Lebiere (2003) also pointed out, "Regrettably, we were not able to state the Newell criteria in such a way that their satisfaction would be entirely a matter of objective fact" (597). Summing up: the Newell test can be used to evaluate, in general, the human-likeness of cognitively inspired computational models and the extent to which such models can be said to have a "theory of cognition". In principle, if we accept the assumption that adequately plausible human-like models can also converge towards human-level results (as has been proven for many computational models in the history of cognitive science), this test could be also seen as an indirect way of assessing the human-level intelligence (in the "weak" sense) of integrated systems. It is, however, difficult to envisage its use in evaluating and comparing specific computational models of cognition (e.g., let's say models of semantic ambiguity resolutions) and, finally, the subjective assignment of the ratings for many of the criteria represents one of its biggest weaknesses.

The Winograd Schema Challenge

In 2012, the computer scientists Hector Levesque, Ernest Davis, and Leora Morgenstern came up with an innovative and brand new challenge to use as a more appropriate test for intelligence. These scholars presented an alternative to the TT, which, as we have seen, suffers from many limitations both as a test of "intelligence" and as a test of the adequacy of a simulative model of cognition. The name of the 2012 test is the Winograd Schema Challenge (named after Terry Winograd, the developer of the SHURDLU system described earlier in the book). The challenge consists of solving referential ambiguity (in particular, the problem of anaphoric pronoun resolution) in a "Winograd schema", which the authors describe as follows: "A pair of sentences differing in only one or two words and containing an ambiguity that is resolved in opposite ways in the two sentences and that requires the use of world knowledge and reasoning for its resolution" (Levesque, Davis, and Morgenstern, 2012: 557). In this context, passing the Winograd Schema Challenge for a program means being able to solve this referential task with "near human levels of success; presumably close to 100%" for a list of collected sentences built according to such schema. In such a collection of sentences, the answer for the pronoun resolution is obvious to humans but cannot be retrieved with classical statistical techniques by machines. Levesque, Davis, and Morgenstern (2012: 554) describe the following four features of the questions used for the challenge:

1 Two parties are mentioned in a sentence by noun phrases. They can be two males, two females, two inanimate objects, or two groups of people or objects.
2 A pronoun or possessive adjective is used in the sentence in reference to one of the parties, but is also of the right sort for the second party. In the case of males, it is "he/him/his"; for females, it is "she/her/her"; for inanimate object it is "it/it/its"; and for groups it is "they/them/their."
3 The question involves determining the referent of the pronoun or possessive adjective. Answer 0 is always the first party mentioned in the sentence (but repeated from the sentence for clarity) and Answer 1 is the second party.
4 There is a word (called the "special word") that appears in the sentence and possibly the question. When it is replaced by another word (called the "alternate word"), everything still makes perfect sense, but the answer changes.

Examples of these questions (divided in two blocks of Winograd Schemas containing two pairs of sentences each) are as follows:

Sentence 1: I poured water from the bottle into the **cup** until **it** was full. What was **full**?

Answer 0: the bottle

Answer 1: the cup

Sentence 2: I poured water from the **bottle** into the cup until **it** was **empty**. What was **empty**?

Answer 0: the bottle

Answer 1: the cup

Sentence 3: Paul tried to call George on the phone but **he** wasn't **successful**. Who was not **successful**?

Answer 0: Paul

Answer 1: George

Sentence 4: Paul tried to call George on the phone but **he** wasn't **available**. Who was not **available**?

Answer 0: Paul

Answer 1: George

As these two blocks of sentences show, in both cases the question asks for a correct disambiguation of the pronouns ("it" and "he" in the examples, respectively) by assigning them to the correct referents in the sentence. It is also evident from these examples that there is always the "special world" used in both the sentence and the question (in the examples, the special and alternate words are "full", "empty", "successful", and "available"). The devised task goes beyond retrieval or statistical matching in large corpora (the authors say that it is "Google-proof": i.e., an automatic system using Google and statistical techniques will not be able to reliably disambiguate these sentences correctly) and requires resorting to some sort of explicit model and reasoning. The main advantages of the Winograd Schema with respect to the TT concerns the fact that: (1) there is no subjectivity involved: the answer is clear from a "human perspective" and the results can be quantitatively and qualitatively evaluated; and (2) the challenge does not require adopting any expert since the wide range of questions concern commonsense knowledge and reasoning that every speaker of a natural language can handle (in this case, English speakers). Some of the weaknesses of the test, however, are the following: the test is, again, language-centric and anthropocentric (as with the original TT), and therefore cannot be considered either a "general" test for intelligence or a general test for human intelligence. In addition, the same behavioural critiques apply here: the mechanisms through which a system can pass the test can be not structurally valid and be completely "functional". As a consequence, the test is not feasible in evaluating simulative models of cognition and cannot be used to ascribe "intelligence" (in the human-like sense) to a system. It can, however, be used to evaluate the human-level performance of the developed systems with respect to the human responses (which for this task is 100%).

Another weakness of the test concerns the binary choice. This artificially reduces the chances of errors for the system (and the chance of success is always at least 50%, which is very high for human-level tasks).

DARPA challenges, RoboCup, and RoboCup@Home

Over the few last decades many diverse robot competitions and challenges – sponsored by different organizations like the DARPA (Defense Advanced Research Projects Agency), the Robot World Cup (RoboCup) Federation, the AAAI (Association for the Advances on Artificial Intelligence), and many others – have been proposed, with the aim of testing the level of development of embodied systems. These competitions have never been proposed as being scientific tests for evaluating the level of "intelligence" in such systems nor their eventual cognitive plausibility. Rather, they have been proposed to evaluate the degree of human-level abilities reached by competing teams working on different systems, platforms, and integrated architectures. As such, they hold a different status with respect to some of the proposals reviewed above. However, they have provided a valuable alternative and have the great merit of creating a community of researchers working together on integrated platforms. One of the most famous events is the DARPA Challenges, a series of competitions sponsored by the DARPA in order to promote the development of autonomous vehicles able to complete, in a limited amount of time, substantial off-road courses. These original challenges (called "Grand Challenges") were later on substituted with different competitions, like the DARPA Urban Challenge, which extended the initial challenge to autonomous operation in a mock urban environment; and, more recently (since 2012), with the DARPA Robotics Challenge, focused on human-supervised robotic technology for disaster-response operations. Another well-known competition, a robot soccer one, known as the Robot World Cup (RoboCup), started in 1997 and has been considered an important testbed for the investigation of cooperative multi-agent systems. Such leagues started with non-humanoid robots but nowadays employ humanoid soccer robots. The stated ultimate goal of RoboCup (www.robocup.org) is described as follows: "By the middle of the 21st century, a team of fully autonomous humanoid robot soccer players shall win a soccer game, complying with the official rules of FIFA, against the winner of the most recent World Cup" (Kitano and Asada, 2000) and, by the year 2030, soccer robots are expected to play competitive games against a team of eight unprofessional players (Gerndt et al., 2015). One thing that has certainly emerged already from the preliminary competitions is the adoption in most teams of hybrid approaches combining low-level reactive systems and higher-level modules for planning and reasoning. This marriage was unavoidable since, as we have seen, certain classes of formalisms and architectures (e.g., those *à la* Brooks) are better suited to dealing with perceptual tasks while others (e.g., the heuristic search methods used in robots, like Shakey, see footnote 20 in Chapter 1) are able to better model high-level phenomena. More recently, the RoboCup organization has proposed a novel competition called the "RoboCup@Home" league that aims to evaluate the level of abilities of assistive robots in domestic applications. So in this case, the idea is one of fostering research on human–robot interaction instead of on multi-agent robot–robot interactions. All these challenges are important testbeds for evaluating the progress and problems of embodied systems showing integrated abilities.

Comparison

The following table provides a synthetic comparison of the main evaluation approaches that have been reviewed so far. For the reasons explicated above about the different intrinsic statuses of the challenges and competitions, such evaluation campaigns are not included (Table 5.1).

The tests considered in the table are: the Turing Test (**TT**); the Turing Test version with the administration of behavioural experiments (**TTwBE**) like the priming effect or others; the Total Turing Test (**TTT**); the Newell Test (**NT**) the Winograd Schema Challenge (**WSC**); and the Minimal Cognitive Grid (**MCG**) proposed in the previous chapters. The MCD is included because – despite not explicitly proposing any kind of test – it represents, nonetheless, as does the "Newell Test", a concrete proposal for the evaluation of the structural accuracy of artificial systems that, however, could in principle additionally be used also to indirectly assess the degree of human-level artificial performances (in particular, thanks to the additional constraints considered for the "performance match" dimension).

The criteria considered for comparing the proposed approaches are those discussed above, namely: the **GT4I** column describes if the approach can be considered a general test for "intelligence"; **T4IHLI** describes if the test allow for a comparison between the results of integrated artificial systems (i.e., systems doing more than one "intelligent" task, not narrow) with human performances (measured in terms of percentage of overlapping positive results) in a way that it is possible to use this behavioural comparison to assess the distance (if any) from human-level performances; and the **T4IHLII** describes if the test can be useful to compare the performances of integrated artificial systems with those exhibited by humans, through evaluating not only the "match" in terms of overlapping positive performances but also, as proposed in the MCG, other psychometric measures like the execution times and type of errors. As a consequence this criterion should allow us to assess the distance (if any) from human-like performances. The columns **T4SHLI** (Test for Specific Human-Level Intelligence) and **T4SHLII** (Test for Specific Human-Like Intelligence) specify, in a narrow setting and for non-multitasking systems, respectively, the considerations about the human level and the human-like performances. The **CA** column is intended to assess whether the analyzed test can be used to evaluate the cognitive adequacy of artificial models (please note that tests able to detect the "human-likeness" of their performances – considering different measures other than just the percentage of success – may not be sufficient for evaluating the cognitive adequacy of

TABLE 5.1 Comparative table of the different evaluation approaches

Tests	GT4I general test for intelligence	T4IHLI test for integrated human-level intellig.	T4IHLII Test for integrated human-like intellig.	T4SHLI test for specific human-level intelligence	T4SHLII test for specific human-like intelligence	CA cogn. adeq.	SE subj evaluat.	QUALE qualit. Evaluat.	QUANE quantit. evaluat.	GE graded evaluat.
Turing test	NO	NO	NO	**YES**	NO	NO	YES	**YES**	NO	NO
Turing test with BE	NO	NO	NO	**YES**	**YES**	NO	YES	**YES**	NO	NO
Total Turing test	NO	**YES**	NO	NO	NO	NO	YES	**YES**	NO	NO
Newell test	NO	MAYBE	**YES**	NO	NO	**YES**	YES	**YES**	NO	**YES**
Winog. schema chall.	NO	NO	NO	**YES**	NO	NO	**NO**	**YES**	**YES**	NO
Minimal cogn. grid	NO	MAYBE	**YES**	MAYBE	**YES**	**YES**	**NO**	**YES**	**YES**	**YES**

a system); the **SE** column evaluates if such tests resort to subjective judgements; the **QUALE** and **QUANE** columns express the type of evaluation allowed by the tests (i.e., qualitative and quantitative); and, finally, the **GE** column indicates whether the system provides the possibility of using only Boolean notions (YES/ NO) or if it allows for the expression of graded rankings and evaluation (in both qualitative or quantitative terms). In bold, the "positive" traits for each of the considered features are represented. In particular, for the **GT4I, it** is considered a positive element of the test, the eventual possibility that it can be used for a "general" test for the intelligence (including non-human intelligences), but none of the proposed approaches is able to tackle this issue. For the **T4IHLI** feature, "YES" is considered the positive option, which describes the possibility of using the performances of the test to evaluate the human-level ability of integrated multitasking systems. A similar discourse holds for the evaluation of the **T4I-HLII, T4SHLI,** and **T4SHLII** criteria. As for the **CA** criterion (obviously not guaranteed by tests interested only in human-level comparisons of the performances of the artificial systems) and the **QUALE, QUANE,** and **GE** criteria, the "YES" option has been considered the positive one. In particular, for the last criterion (GE), the choice of considering "YES" as a positive option depends on the fact that allowing to rank and grade the matching of the performances between humans and systems represents a way to make explicit more subtle differences and similarities both *between* the humans and machines and *within* the different classes of machines built to pass a given test. This criterion is not allowed in any of the variations of the TT (where, at the end, the interrogator must provide a binary YES/NO decision in her/his assessment about the interlocutor) or the Winograd Schema Challenge, though it is built-in to the Newell Test and the MCG. Finally, another considered comparative feature is the **SE**. In this case, of course, the "NO" is considered the positive option since it indicates evaluation methods not based on subjective judgments. As emerges from analyzing the table, the MCG seems to have at its disposal a wider range of positive features compared to the other "evaluation toolkits". In particular, while the YES/NO answers are self-explanatory (since MCG is a graded, non-subjective evaluation tool allowing both quantitative and qualitative analysis about the cognitive adequacy and the human-like performances of artificial systems in both single and multitasking settings) the MAYBE ones suggest that, as anticipated above, the MCG, and in particular its "performance match" dimension, could be also used as an indicator of the eventual human-level performances obtained by an integrated multitasking system or by narrow ones (and the same holds for the Newell test for the T4IHLI feature). Since, however, despite being plausible, an eventual evaluation in this direction has been not yet tested, the columns corresponding to the use of this methodological tool as a means for testing human-level performances of artificial systems have been filled with the MAYBE option and not with the positive "YES" one.

6
THE NEXT STEPS

Abstract
This concluding chapter will synthesize the main issues presented in the book and will try to provide a roadmap for the coming years in the context of cognitive AI research, by suggesting fields where the cognitive design approach can provide valuable inputs for the realization of better AI systems.

The road travelled

In the previous pages of this volume, we introduced and touched upon different themes that have been debated for decades by computer scientists, philosophers, engineers, psychologists, and, more generally, by the scholars working in the interdisciplinary fields of both Artificial Intelligence (AI) and Cognitive Science. The time has come to put some order to the main themes traced in order to identify some of the most relevant ideas conveyed in the book. The first idea concerns the observation that, from a modelling perspective, there is not a definitive "winning" method in the *"science of artificial"* (to use an expression coined by Herbert Simon). As we have seen, indeed, different approaches are useful for modelling certain classes of cognitive phenomena, but no one single approach can account for all aspects of cognition. As a consequence, the road travelled so far suggests that all the different types of models and modelling paradigms are needed and that an important goal for current and future research should consist of individuating how to integrate them in a scientifically principled and non-ad-hoc way. The research area in cognitive architectures, in this respect – given its more than 40 years of experience in the challenges concerning the realization of integrated intelligent systems – could be a field that gains major attention from the AI and cognitive robotics communities (which are nowadays mainly focused on building super "intelligent" and narrow applications). This research area will also certainly retain its central role in the context of the computational cognitive science/cognitive modelling community. The second main idea condensed in the book is that it is not sufficient for an artificial system to obtain human (or super-human) level performances in specific tasks to attach to it the label of a "cognitive system". In particular, we have seen how "functional" systems (in the sense explained in the book) cannot be considered artificial models of cognition if they are not additionally equipped with "structural constraints". As such, they cannot provide any explanatory role with respect to the analogous natural systems executing the same tasks and manifesting the same behaviour. In a period of AI hype and propaganda, driven mainly by the media and the marketing departments of both companies and academia rather than the scientific and technological ones, it is important to keep in mind these very basic, but important, distinctions in order to avoid unfounded conclusions based on the (wrong and manipulated) perception of scientific facts. Among these facts to keep in mind are, at least, the following: (1) we are still far from building machines able to exhibit, in a satisfactory way, human-level abilities (and this is true also if we consider employing machines not as our *"peers"* but just as useful artificial companions; let us consider how minimal − despite the big headlines in newspapers − has been the help provided by robotics and AI systems during the first wave of the COVID-19 crisis); (2) we are still far from understanding many aspects of how the mind and brain work. Of course, some progress has been made in the last few decades, but a full account of this aspect requires more research and joint effort. The third main idea proposed in the book concerns the need for a comparative tool for evaluating the "structural accuracy" of different AI systems (in particular, those biologically or cognitively inspired). Despite the enormous amount of literature devoted to this theme, in fact, a real methodological and practical operationalization of what such an expression really meant is lacking and this has led to tonnes of literature targeting this expression in a way that was much too ambiguous and vaguely defined to have a scientific impact. To fill this gap, I have proposed the Minimal Cognitive Grid (MCG): a simple methodological tool that can be used to practically project and compare different kinds of artificial systems along the "structural accuracy" dimension. As reviewed in the previous chapters, this tool permits the provision of a non-subjective, graded evaluation that allows both quantitative and qualitative analyses about the cognitive adequacy and the human-like performances of artificial systems in both single and multi-tasking settings. In principle (and in prospective), the psychometric characterization of one of its composing dimensions (in particular, the "performance match") could also be useful to evaluate human-level performances in both narrow and unrestricted settings. The fourth idea defended in the book, which was somehow the underlying *fil rouge* of the entire narration, is that in order to avoid the above described myopic euphoria about AI and, on the contrary, in order to make real progress from the scientific point of view, we really need a renewed pact and collaboration between AI and Cognitive Science researchers. In particular, such collaboration is needed both to advance some of the main limitations of modern AI technologies and to improve the understanding of our mental and brain activities via computational simulations. It will probably not be necessary to extend to the two entire fields this collaboration (for example, systems that will not communicate or interact with humans but that will only communicate with other machines do not require any "cognitive interface"), however, there are research areas where the lack of progress is probably due, apart from the intrinsic complexity of the problems needing to be addressed, to the fact that the two areas nowadays do not talk to each other.

The way forward

In the next few pages I will provide some examples of topics where a cognitive approach to the science of the artificial could provide mutual benefits to both the AI and the Cognitive Science communities. I will also provide some pointers to initiatives in this direction that are already in place in the international scientific community. A preliminary general analysis concerning the cognitive design approach (CDA) necessarily involves the individuation of a class of problems where CDA can prove its efficacy in building better machines and better simulative models of cognition. In this respect, evidence from AI research suggests that a place to look at is represented by all those tasks that are particularly easy for humans to but that, on the other hand, are difficult to model in artificial systems. The list of these tasks is transversal and encompasses different research topics within the AI and Cognitive Science communities. A non-exhaustive list would certainly contain – for example – the following ones: machine learning (in particular, the field of *unsupervised learning*), transfer learning, commonsense reasoning (concerning physical, spatial, and action-oriented environments), analogical reasoning, computational creativity, story and narrative understanding, multimodal integration, emotion modelling, dialogues and conversation management in unrestricted settings, decisions explainability, and social cognition abilities relying on notions such as *trust* and *theory of mind* (intended as the capability of understanding other agent's purposes, intentions, and goals).

Let us now zoom in on some of these activities by pointing out how the cognitive design approach can be of help. A primary field of interest concerns the area of cognitively inspired machine learning, which encompasses problems and issues ranging from learning from few or no examples (e.g., few-shot, one-shot, or zero-shot learning) to multimodal integration and transfer learning. From this point of view, among the main characteristics of the learning capability in humans are the relative easiness of learning new knowledge through a limited number of examples and, in addition, the capability of generalizing and mapping what was learnt to other domains. A particularly interesting point of contact between machine learning and the results from experimental research in cognitive science, in particular from developmental psychology, was suggested in a recent paper by Zaadnoordijk, Besold, and Cusack (2020). Here, the authors propose that in order to improve the currently poor performances of systems dealing with unsupervised machine learning (which, as mentioned, is the type of learning obtained with no human supervision), AI engineers and computer scientists should look at how babies acquire their spatial, language, and motor cognitive capabilities in order to endow such AI systems with the possibility of manifesting some forms of ontogenetic development. This general idea is, of course, not new and well rooted in developmental approaches to AI. However, these authors specifically identify five main elements of learning in babies (in particular, babies within the first 12 months of life) that could be used as a possible fruitful focus for machine learning research. Such factors, indeed, are assumed to be the crucial elements enabling infants' quality and speed of learning. The first identified factor concerns the fact that babies' information processing is guided and constrained from birth from their (biological) neural architecture. This means that, similarly, machine learning researchers should find the starting conditions (i.e., the initial training setup) that determine the developmental learning capabilities in different machine learning architectures. The second factor concerns the fact that babies are able to learn statistical relations across diverse, multimodal inputs. Multimodal approaches have already been successfully pursued in machine learning for decades. However, until today, these successes have not caused a widespread shift from unimodal to multimodal training of Deep Neural Networks (DNNs). The third factor is that infants are able to acquire learning in a cumulative way over time while, on the other hand, neural networks (in particular, deep neural networks used in deep learning applications) suffer from the problem known as *catastrophic interference*: a process where new knowledge overwrites, rather than integrates, previous knowledge. Despite the fact that some solutions have been proposed to alleviate this problem, the general issue of catastrophic interference still remains unsolved. This aspect represents a crucial element that needs to be addressed in the current AI research, and insights coming from the way in which babies scaffold, over time, learned knowledge can be really crucial to provide technical insights. The fourth factor identified is that learning in infants does not happen in a passive way and, similarly, more interdisciplinary efforts should be done in the context of so-called "active learning" and "curiosity-driven learning". Finally, the fifth factor concerns the fact that learning in babies is also the result of interactions with other agents. This fact should represent a call for doing machine learning research *"out of the vacuum"* and in more ecological settings; i.e., machine learning systems should be studied within a societal context of interacting agents (which can be humans or other artificial systems). This aspect has been also recently considered within the "cognitive AI" community with the proposal of the so-called Interactive Task Learning (Laird et al., 2017). This task consists of allowing an artificial system to learn the underlying elements of a task (rather than how to optimally solve it) via a natural interactions with humans, used as instructors in a typical student-teacher situation. The overall idea of this relatively new field of investigation is that the task to be learnt can be described (via natural language or physical activity, e.g., by pointing to objects in an environment) such that its overall purpose, the appropriate "moves", and its goal and termination conditions can be internalized by an artificial system. The "student" (i.e., the artificial system, in our case) can ask specific questions to the instructor (e.g., a human) to assess that the internal representation of the tasks that it is building is actually the correct one. Finally, after the system is able to understand the essence of the task, it can learn how to execute it well. This example goes exactly in the direction suggested by Zaadnoordijk, Besold, and Cusack (2020) and would require a robust campaign of experiments to show the limitations of the current systems in this ecological setting.

If we switch our attention to a different area, we can explore a similar discourse. For example, let us consider the context of story and narrative understanding. Since the beginning of early AI research, cognitive scientists like Shank and Abelson (with the introduction of the "script" notion) unveiled the role of story-centred data structures as building blocks for the realization of dialogue and narrative understanding systems. Still, nowadays, cognitive science research plays (and has played) a major role in the development of one of the most advanced narrative AI technologies: the Genesis system developed by Patrick Henry Winston and his collaborators at MIT (Winston, 2012a, 2014). This system analyzes stories in textual formats and is able to provide short summaries with an incredible level of synthesis. The system implements the Strong Story Hypothesis: a theoretical view that, according to Winston, frames the reason for why humans are smarter than other primates by hypothesizing that story understanding (and storytelling) plays a central role in human intelligence (Winston, 2011, 2012b). At the heart of the story-understanding mechanisms of Genesis are few commonsense rules that are able to extract explicit representations of events from texts and materialize some implicit connections within a plot. This area of research represents a quite straightforward example of the benefits of collaboration between AI and Cognitive Science scholars (Winston, who passed away in 2019, was one of the rare scholars able to do research in both fields). This is an example that should be encouraged and reinforced to improve current AI technologies.[1] By mentioning Winston's research, we have also touched on two other important topics that still would benefit from a cognitively inspired approach: the research area on commonsense reasoning and the one on natural language understanding. Concerning the former: we have already seen (in Chapter 2) that this is a very old problem within the AI agenda. Nonetheless, many logic-oriented approaches (ranging from fuzzy logic to default logics to all the different proposals of

---

1 Along this line, Patrick Winston, together with the computational linguist Mark Alan Finlayson – his former Ph.D. student at MIT – promoted, from 2009 to 2016, a series of workshops called "Computational Models of Narratives", partly financed by DARPA, which became a reference point for scholars working in this field http://narrative.csail.mit.edu/. I co-organized with Finlayson and other international scholars (Ben Miller, Rémi Ronfard, and Stephen Ware) the 2015 and 2016 editions of the workshop (http://narrative.csail.mit.edu/cmn15/ and http://narrative.csail.mit.edu/cmn16/).

non-monotonic logics) have mostly failed to provide a suitable solution, due to the intrinsic computational complexity of their reasoning procedure (ranging from undecidability to intractability, according to the different versions of proposed formalisms). Only recently have we been able to assist the development, under certain strict specific assumptions, of non-monotonic reasoning frameworks able to reach the same complexity of standard deductive reasoning procedures (e.g., see Giordano et al., 2020, for a review) or a polynomial time complexity (see Bonatti et al., 2015). However commonsense reasoning is really an ubiquitous tasks in humans, an everyday activity, and in addition, these achievements are not sufficient to account for its linear and real-time execution. In other words, by using the previously introduced "dual process" terminology proposed by Kahneman, commonsense reasoning processes are mostly Type 1 processes since they operate in a very fast way. On the other hand, most of the logics proposed to handle this phenomenon have a complexity that is higher than standard deductive processes (i.e., belonging to Type 2 processes). The poor performances of current AI systems in commonsense reasoning (involving not just natural language or question answering but also systems dealing with temporal, physical, and visual reasoning tasks) has also been recently pointed out in a detailed review by Davis and Marcus (2015). Therefore, it is striking to see how, despite this being a well-known problem since the early days of AI, we have not seen much progress on this topic. It is also clear, however, how being able to produce human-level solutions for this challenge represents a crucial research goal for AI researchers to achieve. The complexity of this task also suggests a strong interdisciplinary effort. The advantages are quite evident: Cognitive Science can provide AI with knowledge about heuristics to implement in commonsense reasoning systems, cognitively inspired AI systems can provide insights about the dynamics (which are not visible through neuroscience experiments nor psychological ones) of the interaction between the different commonsense heuristics put in place in a machine, thus providing a computational ground to test theories and individuate eventual theoretical "bugs" to fix (as the case of the DUAL PECCS systems shows). Commonsense reasoning represents also one of the main problems of current natural language processing (NLP) systems. Let us consider, for our purposes, the most recent and advanced technology in the field: the GPT-3, announced in May 2020 by researchers from OpenAI (Brown et al., 2020). GPT-3 is a new deep-learning model (built by scraping the web) with around 175 billion parameters. The model achieves state-of-the-art performance across a variety of NLP tasks. Training the model, however, is so expensive that it could not be retrained to fix an eventual bug (retraining with half a trillion words costs – according to an estimate –$12 million). The neural network model, indeed, is so large that it cannot easily be moved off the cluster of machines it was trained on (and this leads to a problem that we could call "gigantic immobility"). Now, these simple data alone can give an idea of how far a model of this type is from the considerations that we have raised above. In particular, a language model of this type cannot learn new knowledge and be updated, does not develop itself over time, is completely ungrounded on any kind of biological or cognitively inspired constraint, and, definitively, is galaxies away from understanding anything and from being comparable to an infant's ability of learning and grasping the foundations of language. The incredible performances showed by the GPT-3 model in NLP tasks are, indeed, obtained thanks to the incredible computational power demanded and adopted for its usage. The cost of handling such an unconstrained and gigantic model, however, is unsustainable in all possible ways (e.g., both economically and environmentally, due to the high energy consumption of such a system). In addition, as with its predecessors, the model seems to fall short in dealing with the foundational issues of natural language understanding and, as in the cases analyzed previously in the book, the super-human performances are accompanied by subhuman-like errors in tasks of commonsense and analogical reasoning. In this respect, a caveat must be mentioned: the latter mentioned experiments are only preliminary and unsystematic[2] (and, as such, need to be scientifically and extensively validated in order to have scientific relevance). Nonetheless, they seem to confirm the classical limitations of this type of system. In particular, Davis and Marcus report – at this link: https://cs.nyu.edu/faculty/davise/papers/GPT3CompleteTests.html – a whole set of examples used in their experiments with GPT-3 on commonsense reasoning involving different kinds of abilities,[3] while Melanie Mitchell has described in a *Medium* article[4] her experiments on analogical reasoning by comparing GPT-3 to the notorious system CopyCat, developed by Douglas Hofstadter and colleagues (including Mitchell) at MIT in the 1980s and 1990s (Hofstadter and Mitchell, 1995). Of course, as mentioned, these preliminary and unsystematic experiments cannot be considered scientific evidence of the inability of GPT-3 to deal with commonsense or analogical reasoning (also because in many cases the reported answers are correct), however, the types or errors produced reveal, *in nuce*, some classical misalignment between functional AI systems and human performance. Such initial hints, however, need to be confirmed or disproved by extensive and systematic evaluation campaigns. A fact that certainly emerges and doesn't need any additional analysis, however, concerns the complete lack of "transparency" in this model as to why certain errors are made or answers provided. Previously (in Chapter 1) we called this the "opacity" problem and we have already mentioned how this is a foundational element that affects connectionist systems, in general, and that explodes with deep learning architectures. The call for transparency and accountability of algorithmic procedures is, however, not only an important desideratum for human–machine

---

2 The reasons behind the lack of systematic results are different. The first one concerns the fact the software has been announced very recently, in respect to the time of writing this. The second one concerns the fact that GPT-3 is currently (as of September 2020) accessible only via Application Programming Interface (API) and that this access has been provided to a minimal set of researchers around the world, selected on a discretional basis by OpenAI.

3 A synthesis is provided in an *MIT Technology Review* article: https://www.technologyreview.com/2020/08/22/1007539/gpt3-openai-language-generator-artificial-intelligence-ai-opinion/.

4 https://medium.com/@melaniemitchell.me/follow-up-to-can-gpt-3-make-analogies-b202204bd292.

interaction. In certain cases, e.g., in Europe, it is now also a mandatory requirement, requested by the novel legislation on privacy known by the acronym "GDPR" (General Data Protection Regulation) that has been in effect since 2018. GDPR, indeed, explicitly calls for the "right to an explanation" for the decisions made by automatic systems. This has led to the development of a brand new field called Explainable AI (or XAI, see footnote 4 in Chapter 3).[5] However, the problem here is what kind of explanations do humans need in order to make intelligible the underlying decision strategies used by artificial systems? Again: Cognitive Science can help in this respect. The first hint coming from this field, indeed, is that humans look for causal explanations (i.e., a very restrictive type of mechanistic explanations, see Chapter 3). The importance of causality in human reasoning (and in AI) has been championed by Turing Award winner Judea Pearl (Pearl, 2009; Pearl and Mackenzie, 2018). The extrapolation of causal cues in systems like deep neural networks, however, is far from being solved, as Pearl warns. Apart from the extraction of causal cues, however, there are other cognitive traits that should be taken into account in XAI systems (at least in those that revolve around final users as their direct targets). For example, the fact that humans look for selected explanations, i.e., due to our limitations we do not want to be presented with the whole chain of causal connections explaining a given algorithmic decision (since this would require, in certain cases, managing too many unintelligible variables). We want a synthetic explanation that gets to the core of the causal chain. Also, the mechanisms behind the individuation of such selections, however, are not known and would require closer collaboration between AI and Cognitive Science researchers. Another cognitively effective explanatory cue concerns the use of contrastive explanations (see Miller, 2019): people do not ask why event P happened, but rather why event P happened instead of some event Q. This aspect should be embedded in systems interacting with end-users. Finally, explanations are a social element in human–human interactions. So, including them in a narrative and argumentative framework would facilitate their comprehensibility to human users.[6] The implementation of all these characteristics in AI systems have huge potential but, again, require close collaboration between researchers working in the two fields (or at their intersection). A similar discourse holds for systems capable of analogical reasoning. There are actually very few systems able, to a certain extent, to deal with this crucial cognitive capability. Apart from the previously mentioned pioneering CopyCat system, the most advanced in this respect is

5 Actually this field of investigation it is not really new (only its name is), since the quest for providing human-understandable explanations of algorithmic decisions was already the battle field of the experts systems and the case-based reasoning community.
6 Antonis Kakas and Loizos Michael are two of the most active researchers in the AI community who argue for the need for a cognitive approach to argumentation and explanation frameworks (Kakas and Michael, 2016) and who have proposed, in the last few years, a number of tutorials and events at major AI conferences on this theme. E.g., see http://cognition.ouc.ac.cy/argument/ and http://cognition.ouc.ac.cy/cognitar/index.html.

the Companions Cognitive Architecture developed by Ken Forbus and colleagues, and formed by a triplet of software components known as the Structure Mapping Engine (SME), MAC/FAC system for similarity based retrieval, and the SAGE system for generalization (Forbus and Hinrich, 2017). Unsurprisingly, this system is built using a structural design approach based on a theoretically driven decomposition of the processes being simulated and, in particular, on the implementation of the Structure-Mapping Theory (Gentner, 1983), which sees analogy as a knowledge-mapping and transfer process from a base domain to a target domain. Analogy and computational analogical reasoning should also be an area that machine learning researchers should look at more closely, in order to deal with the problem of transfer learning that affect their models. Analogies are also important in the context of automatic knowledge discovery[7] and creative invention of novel knowledge and can be crucially implemented also in AI systems operating in the context of "computational creativity" research. This subfield of AI research is currently open to both cognitively inspired and machine-oriented approaches (see e.g., Augello et al., 2016; Lieto et al., 2019; Veale and Cardoso, 2019; Chiodino et al., 2020) for building systems able to exhibit creative traits when involved in tasks requiring what Margaret Boden calls transformational, exploratory, and combinatorial creative processes (Boden, 2009). The overall impression is that, for the field of AI in general, the invention or authentic "artificial styles" (e.g., in diverse artistic domains) requires something more than what is available nowadays. Creativity, however, is not only a matter of artistic domains. When we find a novel solution for solving an everyday problem, we also exploit the potential of our creative thinking. In this respect, the vast amount of literature on cognitive research about creative problem solving (in human and animal cognition) could be very useful for building creative machines. The quest for computational creativity, however, also requires considering additional elements: (computational models of) emotions that are a driving force of our decisions and meta-cognitive capabilities (Damasio, 1994); and the fact that creativity happens in a social context and, as such, must intercept, interpret, and abstract in insightful way what happens in a multi-agent societal setting. For the first aspect, it is well known that current research on effective computing in AI could benefit from insights from psychological studies on emotion (Picard, 1997). However – with a few notable exceptions of systems like SenticNet (Cambria et al., 2020), developed by Erik Cambria and colleagues at the NTU and explicitly adopting psychological models of emotion (Susanto et al. 2020) to conduct sentiment analysis[8] – most current research in the field is focused

---

7 An important sub-area of this historical field of AI is the one of automatic scientific discovery, championed by the protagonists of the cognitivist tradition like Pat Langley and his pioneering BACON system (Langley, Bradshaw, and Simon, 1983). An updated view on the field is provided in Langley (2019).

8 Sentiment analysis is a subfield of affective computing aiming at automatically individuating the driving sentiment or mood in pieces of texts.

on the multimodal recognition of human emotions from physical states (e.g., from face recognition or computer vision systems or from wearable devices) by using standard machine learning techniques and with little research done on emotion-driven decisions and appraisal. Within the same context of "sentiment analysis", in fact, the focus is on building very shallow models that are able to classify, after an extensive phase of manual annotation, the "positive" vs. "negative" polarity of texts without any grounding and grasping of the emotional content expressed therein and also without providing significant findings in the context of natural language processing research (this field is mainly driven by business needs rather than scientific ones). In the context of cognitive architecture and robotics, on the other hand, computational models of emotions have been more accurately devised and adopted within agents architectures in order to inform the processing mechanisms of intelligent systems. Some of these architectures (e.g., the H-CogAff architecture developed by Sloman and colleagues, see Sloman, 2001, 2002) have shown, in accordance with psychological theories, how emotions are not a unitary phenomenon and are not all the same. The neuroscientist Antonio Damasio (1994: 131–134), for example, suggests that there are primary and secondary emotions, while Sloman (1998) suggests including tertiary emotions as well. Apart from the terminology, the difference between such variances of emotional states lies in the type of processes involved in their manifestation (ranging from physiological reactions to higher forms of semantically rich, affective states). While the first type of emotional reactive responses can be somehow detected and reproduced by shallow models, secondary and tertiary emotions require more sophisticated meta-management activities. Emotion modelling and recognition has played and still plays an important role in the context of social robotics. The first social robot ever realized was Kismet, developed by Cynthia Breazeal (Breazeal and Scassellati, 2000; Breazeal, 2004) at MIT. This robot was the first one able to demonstrate a wide repertoire of emotional behaviours, able to engage humans in an interaction. Nowadays, most social robotic platforms currently used (like Pepper or the iCub) have a more stylized humanoid shape (in the case of iCub, the shape resembles that of a little child). Still these platforms are mainly focused on the perceptual task of assigning an emotional label to certain visual or auditory signals or individuating some low-level social cues (e.g., gaze following) that require the interplay of perception, attention, and memory modules. However, more complex social interactions (such as building rapport, negotiation, etc.) require the interplay of additional modules such as emotion/motivation information processing modules, metacognition, and language, just to name a few. The gap to fill, therefore, concerns – once again – the integration of perceptual level social cues with higher order meta-cognitive functions that would allow considering emotions a real driver for human-like decision making. This would enable a more natural human–robot interaction that can take place over longer time scales (days, weeks, and months: what Newell calls the "Social Band") and would extend our interaction with machines to crucial notions such as cooperation, collective-action, theory of mind, and trust (Castelfranchi and Falcone, 2010).

Towards a standard model of mind/common model of cognition

One of the most interesting developments of the last decade within the fields of cognitive AI and cognitive modelling research is represented by the proposal of a Standard Model of Mind (later on called the Common Model of Cognition) by John Laird, Christian Lebiere, and Paul Rosenbloom (Laird, Lebiere, and Rosenbloom, 2017). The idea of these three researchers was one of abstracting, from some of the most adopted cognitive architectures that they have developed – namely, SOAR, ACT-R, and SIGMA[9] – a sort of ideal model (a standard one) about the underlying common architectural elements that human-like minds should possess. This abstraction is based on the consensus reached in the community over decades of research and on the convergence reached by these three systems that, despite starting from different assumptions about the architecture of human cognition, have converged towards some interesting commonalities. The areas of consensus reached by such diverse architectures have been grouped into different levels of analysis: (i) Structure and Processing mechanisms, (ii) Memory and Content; (iii) Learning processes, and (iv) Perception and Motor Mechanisms. Concerning the first, an important element of consensus regards the fact that processing in human-like architecture is assumed to be based on a small number of task-independent modules and should support both serial and parallel information processing mechanisms (parallel between modules and serial within them). From an architectural perspective, all the three architectures taken as a source of inspiration for the design of the Common Model converge towards the necessity of distinguishing between a Long-Term Declarative Memory and a Procedural one, as well as the necessity of a working memory module operating as a control interface between the Procedural module and other modules such as the Declarative Memory and the Perception/Motor modules. Concerning the Memory and Content issues, the main point of convergence regards the integration of hybrid symbolic–subsymbolic representations and processing and the inclusion of relevant metadata like frequency, recency, similarity, activation, etc. attached to the processed representations (neural, symbolic, or hybrid). The fact that such integration is necessary is nowadays widely accepted and, indeed, classical symbolic architectures like SOAR are also moving towards hybridization. As for the learning part, the elements of convergence regard the following assumptions: (i) all types of long-term knowledge (i.e., knowledge shared in one of the two long-term memories) should be learnable from a human-like architecture, (ii) learning is seen an incremental processes typically based on some form of a backward flow of information through internal representations

---

9 Sigma is a novel cognitive architecture that starts with the same basic assumption of SOAR (Rosenbloom, 2013) but that uses probabilistically graphical models, in particular factor graphs, as representational elements in its long-term memory, working memory, and perceptual and motor components. In general, the graphical models can be considered a class of symbolic representations, where the relations between concepts are weighted by their strength, calculated through statistical computations.

of past experiences, and (iii) learning over longer time scales is assumed to arise from the accumulation of learning over short-term experiences. Finally, in regards to the perceptual and motor parts (the least developed, with respect to the others), the main points of consensus are limited to the fact that perceptual and motor modules are assumed to be modality specific (e.g., auditory, visual, etc.) and associated with specific buffers for the access to the working memory. Since all these points of convergence have been reached by starting from completely diverse assumptions, these findings are somewhat surprising and worth investigating. The Standard Model of Mind, however, is currently highly underspecified, as the authors themselves admit. It represents a starting point, a platform for developing high-profile research in both AI and (computational) Cognitive Science. These two disciplines, in fact, can find in projects like this a way to join forces and this can be done in light of a new mutual interest and convenience. While, indeed, AI technology has reached important levels of performance in narrow settings, the missing part concerns exactly the study of how to create artificial companions (embodied and disembodied) that are able to integrate different skills in order to help humans in their everyday activities. Similarly, computational Cognitive Science is interested in individuating how the brain and mind work as integrated systems. This renewed convergence is, in my view, a necessity driven by the fact that modern and future AI and Cognitive Science research will be once again disciplines interested in the same topic: namely, the discovery of the mechanisms that enable multitasking intelligence. In order to advance scientific knowledge in their respective fields, in fact, they need to evolve and become sciences (of the artificial) that study the mysteries of integrated intelligence. The time seems ripe for such a renewed collaboration.

Community

Scientific advancements are impossible to obtain without a community of people targeting, with different approaches, the same problems. That's why I want to conclude this book by pointing out some of the main recurrent events that, in the last decade, have enabled the development of a community of researchers around the world that discusses in detail the issues presented in this book. Apart from the main scientific meetings in the respective AI and Cognitive Science communities (like the Annual Meeting of the Cognitive Science Society – CogSci – or the International Conference on Cognitive Modelling – ICCM – for the Cognitive Science side; and the International Joint Conference on Artificial Intelligence – IJCAI – and the International Conference Artificial Intelligence – AAAI – for the AI field) there have been many scientific events and initiatives that have targeted topics and issues, and asking for a renewed collaboration between the AI and Cognitive Science disciplines. In the area of Cognitive Robotics, a particularly active role of promoting such research themes is undertaken by the IEEE Technical Committee on Cognitive Robotics (www.ieee-ras.org/cognitive-robotics/). In regards to the scientific meetings: the international conference series on

Cognitive Systems (ACS) (www.cogsys.org) has played and continues to play an important role in the United States for promoting this type of research. A similar role is played in Europe by the AIC workshop series on "Artificial Intelligence and Cognition", started in 2013 (www.aicworkshopseries.org). Other relevant international venues explicitly addressing the issues covered in this book are the BICA Conference (the International Conference on Biologically Inspired Cognitive Architectures) and the EUCognition conference series (now ended), as well as the annual AAAI Symposia that often host events revolving around the issues discussed in this book (the discussion around the Standard Model of Mind/ Common Model of Cognition started in a 2013 AAAI symposium and was later on expanded upon in two separate AAAI symposia in 2017 and 2018). Hopefully, in the future this community of cross-disciplinary researchers will grow, in order to face the scientific challenges that AI and Cognitive Science should answer. As we have seen, leaving the propaganda aside, there is still a lot to do.

REFERENCES

Anderson, J. R., Bothell, D., Byrne, M. D., Douglass, S., Lebiere, C., & Qin, Y. (2004). An integrated theory of the mind. *Psychological Review*, 111(4), 1036.

Anderson, J. R., & Lebiere, C. (2003). The Newell test for a theory of cognition. *Behavioral and Brain Sciences*, 26(5), 587–601.

Anderson, J. R., & Betz, J. (2001). A hybrid model of categorization. *Psychonomic Bulletin & Review*, 8(4), 629–647.

Anderson, J. R. (1990). *The Adaptive Character of Thought*. New York: Psychology Press.

Arbib, M. A. (2018). From cybernetics to brain theory, and more: A memoir. *Cognitive Systems Research*, 50, 83–145.

Arbib, M. A. (ed.). (2002). *The Handbook of Brain Theory and Neural Networks*. MIT Press.

Augello, A., Infantino, I., Lieto, A., Pilato, G., Rizzo, R., & Vella, F. (2016). Artwork creation by a cognitive architecture integrating computational creativity and dual process approaches. *Biologically Inspired Cognitive Architectures*, 15, 74–86.

Ball, J., Rodgers, S., & Gluck, K. (2004). Integrating ACT-R and Cyc in a large-scale model of language comprehension for use in intelligent agents. In *AAAI Workshop* (pp. 19–25).

Bartlett, F. (1958). *Thinking: An Experimental and Social Study*. Allen and Unwin.

Bermudez, J. L. (2005). *Philosophy of Psychology*. London and New York: Routledge.

Bernoulli, D. (1954). Exposition of a new theory on the measurement of risk. *Econometrica*, 22(1), 23–36.

Blouw, P., Solodkin, E., Thagard, P., & Eliasmith, C. (2016). Concepts as semantic pointers: A framework and computational model. *Cognitive Science*, 1128–1162.

Boden, M. A. (2009). Computer models of creativity. *AI Magazine*, 30(3), 23–23.

Bonatti, P. A., Faella, M., Petrova, I. M., & Sauro, L. (2015). A new semantics for overriding in description logics. *Artificial Intelligence*, 222, 1–48.

Bossaerts, P., Yadav, N., & Murawski, C. (2019). Uncertainty and computational complexity. *Philosophical Transactions of the Royal Society B: Biological Sciences*, 374(1766), 20180138.

Braitenberg, V. (1986). *Vehicles: Experiments in Synthetic Psychology*. MIT Press.

Bringsjord, S. (2011). Psychometric artificial intelligence. *Journal of Experimental & Theoretical Artificial Intelligence*, 23(3), 271–277.

Breazeal, C. L. (2004). *Designing Sociable Robots*. MIT Press.

Breazeal, C. L., & Scassellati, B. (2000). Infant-like social interactions between a robot and a human caretaker. *Adaptive Behavior*, 8(1), 1–43.

Brooks, R. A. (1999). *Cambrian Intelligence: The Early History of the New AI*. MIT Press.

Brooks, R. A. (1991). Intelligence without representation. *Artificial Intelligence*, 47(1–3), 139–159.

Brooks, R. (1986). A robust layered control system for a mobile robot. *IEEE Journal on Robotics and Automation*, 2(1), 14–23.

Brown, T. B., Mann, B., Ryder, N., Subbiah, M., Kaplan, J., Dhariwal, P., ... Agarwal, S. (2020). Language models are few-shot learners. *arXiv preprint arXiv:2005.14165*.

Cambria E., Li Y., Xing F., Poria S., Kwok K. (2020). SenticNet 6: Ensemble Application of Symbolic and Subsymbolic AI for Sentiment Analysis. In *Conference on Information and Knowledge Management (CIKM)*, (pp. 105–114).

Cangelosi, A., & Parisi, D. (eds.). (2012). *Simulating the Evolution of Language*. Springer Science & Business Media.

Castelfranchi, C., & Falcone, R. (2010). *Trust Theory: A Socio-cognitive and Computational Model* (Vol. 18). John Wiley & Sons.

Chater, N., Oaksford, M., Nakisa, R., & Redington, M. (2003). Fast, frugal, and rational: How rational norms explain behavior. *Organizational Behavior and Human Decision Processes*, 90(1), 63–86.

Chater, N., & Oaksford, M. (1999). Ten years of the rational analysis of cognition. *Trends in Cognitive Sciences*, 3(2), 57–65.

Chiodino, E., Lieto, A., Perrone, F., & Pozzato, G. L. (2020). A goal-oriented framework for knowledge invention and creative problem solving in cognitive architectures. *Proceedings of ECAI 2020*, (Vol. 2020, 2893–2894).

Chiodino, E., Di Luccio, D., Lieto, A., Messina, A., Pozzato, G. L., & Rubinetti, D. (2020). A knowledge-based system for the dynamic generation and classification of novel contents in multimedia broadcasting. In *Proceedings of ECAI* 2020 (Vol. 2020, pp. 680–687).

Chomsky, N. (1957). *Syntactic Structures*. Mouton & Co.

Churchland, P. S., & Sejnowski, T. J. (1992). *The Computational Brain*. Cambridge, MA: MIT Press.

Churchland, P. M., & Churchland, P. S. (1990). Could a machine think? Recent arguments and new prospects, *Scientific American*, 262(1), 32–37.

Copeland, B. J. (2000). The turing test. *Minds and Machines*, 10, 519–539.

Cordeschi, R., & Frixione, M. (2007). Computationalism under attack. In *Cartographies of the Mind* (pp. 37–49). Dordrecht: Springer.

Cordeschi, R. (2002). *The Discovery of the Artificial: Behavior, Mind and Machines Before and Beyond Cybernetics*. Berlin and New York: Springer. doi:10.1007/978-94-015-9870-5.

Cordeschi, R. (1991). The discovery of the artificial: Some protocybernetic developments, 1930–1940. *AI & Society*, 5, 218–238.

Crick, F. (1989). The recent excitement about neural networks. *Nature*, 337, 129–32.

Damasio, A. (1994). *Descartes' Error: Emotion, Reason, and the Human Brain Paperback*.

Davis, E., & Marcus, G. (2015). Commonsense reasoning and commonsense knowledge in artificial intelligence. *Communications of the ACM*, 58(9), 92–103.

de Melo, C. M., & Terada, K. (2019). Cooperation with autonomous machines through culture and emotion. *PloS One*, 14(11), e0224758.

Dennett, D. C. (1988). *The Intentional Stance*. Cambridge, MA: Bradford Books and MIT Press.

Dennett, D. C. (1986). Is there an autonomous 'knowledge level'? In Z. W. Pylyshyn & W. Demopoulos (eds.), *Meaning and Cognitive Structure: Issues in the Computational Theory of Mind*. Norwood, NJ: Ablex.

Dennett, D. C. (1976). *Brainstorms: Philosophical Essays on Mind and Psychology*. Montgomery, VT: Bradford Books.

Derbinsky, N., Laird, J. E., & Smith, B. (2010). Towards efficiently supporting large symbolic declarative memories. In *Proceedings of the 10th international conference on cognitive modeling* (pp. 49–54).

Dreyfus, H. (1972). *What Computers Can't Do: The Limits of Artificial Intelligence*. MIT Press.

Eliasmith, C., Stewart, T. C., Choo, X., Bekolay, T., DeWolf, T., Tang, Y., & Rasmussen, D. (2012). A large-scale model of the functioning brain. *Science*, 338(6111), 1202–1205.

Epstein, R., Roberts, G., & Beber, G. (eds.). (2009). *Parsing the Turing Test*. The Netherlands: Springer.

Ericsson, K. A., & Simon, H. A. (1980). Verbal reports as data. *Psychological Review*, 87(3), 215.

Ferrucci, D., Levas, A., Bagchi, S., Gondek, D., & Mueller, E. T. (2013). Watson: Beyond jeopardy! *Artificial Intelligence*, 199, 93–105.

Fikes, R. E., Hart, P. E., & Nilsson, N. J. (1972). Learning and executing generalized robot plans. *Artificial Intelligence*, 3(4), 251–288.

Fodor, J. A., & Pylyshyn, Z. W. (1988). Connectionism and cognitive architecture: A critical analysis, *Cognition*, 28, 3–71.

Fodor, J. A. (1986). Why paramecia don't have mental representations. *Midwest Studies in Philosophy*, 10, 3–23.

Forbes, N. (2004). *Imitation of Life: How Biology Is Inspiring Computing*. Cambridge, MA: MIT Press.

Forbus, K. D., & Hinrich, T. (2017). Analogy and relational representations in the companion cognitive architecture. *AI Magazine*, 38(4), 34–42.

Franklin, S. (1995). *Artificial Minds*. MIT Press.

French R. (1990). Subcognition and the limits of the turing test, *Mind*, 99, 53–65.

Friedman, D., Isaac, R. M., James, D., & Sunder, S. (2014). *Risky Curves: On the Empirical Failure of Expected Utility*. New York: Routledge.

Frixione, M. (2015). The turing test and the interface problem: A role for the imitation game in the methodology of cognitive science. *PARADIGMI*. 129–148.

Frixione, M. (2001). Tractable competence. *Minds and Machines*, 11(3), 379–397.

Gärdenfors, P. (2000). *Conceptual Spaces: The Geometry of Thought*. Cambridge, MA: MIT Press.

Gardner, H. (2011). *Frames of Mind: The Theory of Multiple Intelligences*. Hachette UK.

Gentner, D. (1983). Structure-mapping: A theoretical framework for analogy. *Cognitive Science*, 7(2), 155–170. doi:10.1207/ s15516709cog0702_3.

Gerndt, R., Seifert, D., Baltes, J. H., Sadeghnejad, S., & Behnke, S. (2015). Humanoid robots in soccer: Robots versus humans in RoboCup 2050. *IEEE Robotics & Automation Magazine*, 22(3), 147–154.

Gigerenzer, G. (2019). How to explain behavior?. *Topics in cognitive science*, 12(4), 1363–1381.

Gigerenzer, G., Hertwig, R., & Pachur, T. (eds.). (2011). *Heuristics: The Foundations of Adaptive Behavior* (p. xx). New York: Oxford University Press.

Gigerenzer, G. (2000). *Adaptive Thinking: Rationality in the Real World*. Oxford: Oxford University Press.

Gigerenzer, G., & Todd, P. M. (1999). *Simple Heuristics that Make Us Smart*. Oxford University Press.

Giordano, L., Gliozzi, V., Lieto, A., Olivetti, N., & Pozzato, G. L. (2020). Reasoning about typicality and probabilities in preferential description logics. In *Applications and Practices in Ontology Design, Extraction and Reasoning, Studies on Semantic Web*. IOS Press. *arXiv preprint arXiv:2004.09507*.

Goldstein, D. G., & Gigerenzer, G. (2002). Models of ecological rationality: The recognition heuristic. *Psychological Review*, 109(1), 75.

Goodfellow, I., Bengio, Y., Courville, A., & Bengio, Y. (2016). *Deep Learning* (Vol. 1). Cambridge, MA: MIT Press.

Griffiths, T. L., Lieder, F., & Goodman, N. D. (2015). Rational use of cognitive resources: Levels of analysis between the computational and the algorithmic. *Topics in Cognitive Science*, 7(2), 217–229.

Grossberg, S. (1976). Adaptive pattern classification and universal recoding: I. Parallel development and coding of neural feature detectors. *Biological Cybernetics*, 23:121–34.

Harnad, S. (1990). The symbol grounding problem. *Physica D*, 42, 335–346.

Hart, P. E., Nilsson, N. J., & Raphael, B. (1968). A formal basis for the heuristic determination of minimum cost paths in graphs. *IEEE Transactions on Systems Science and Cybernetics SSC*, 4(2), 100–107.

Hawkins, J., & Blakeslee, S. (2005). *On Intelligence*. New York: Times Books.

Hebb, D. O. (1949). *The Organization of Behavior*. New York and London: Wiley and Chapman.

Hempel, C., & Oppenheim, P. (1948). Studies in the Logic of Explanation. *Philosophy of Science*, 15, 135–175. Reprinted in Hempel, 245–290, 1965.

Hofstadter, D. R., & Mitchell, M. (1995). The copycat project: A model of mental fluidity and analogy-making. *Advances in Connectionist and Neural Computation Theory*, 2, 205–267.

Holland. J. (1975). *Adaptation in Natural and Artificial Systems*. University of Michigan Press.

Hopfield, J. J. (1982). Neural networks and physical systems with emergent collective computational abilities. *Proceedings of the National Academy of Sciences of USA*, 79, 2554–2558.

Horvitz, E. J., Cooper, G. F., & Heckerman, D. E. (1989). Reflection and action under scarce resources: Theoretical principles and empirical study. *IJCAI*, 2, 1121–1127.

Hsu, F.-H. (1999). "IBM's deep blue chess grandmaster chips", IEEE Micro, Los Alamitos, CA, USA. *IEEE Computer Society*, 19(2), 70–81.

Jean, S., Cho, K., Memisevic, R., & Bengio, Y. (2015). On using very large target vocabulary for neural machine translation. *Proc. ACL-IJCNLP, arXiv preprint arXiv:1412.2007*.

Johnson-Laird, P. N. (2006). *How We Reason*. Oxford University Press, USA.

Kahneman, D. (2011). *Thinking, Fast and Slow*. London: Allen Lane.

Kakas, A. C., & Michael, L. (2016). Cognitive systems: Argument and cognition. *IEEE Intelligent Informatics Bulletin*, 17(1), 14–20.

Kitano, H., & Asada, M. (2000). The RoboCup humanoid challenge as the millennium challenge for advanced robotics. *Advanced Robotics*, 13(8), 723–736.

Kitano, H., Hamahashi, S., & Luke, S. (1998). The perfect *C. elegans* project: An initial report, *Artificial Life*, 4, 141–156.

Kotseruba, I., & Tsotsos, J. K. (2020). 40 years of cognitive architectures: Core cognitive abilities and practical applications. *Artificial Intelligence Review*, 53(1), 17–94.

LaCurts, K. (2011). Criticisms of the turing test and why you should ignore (most of) them. In *Philosophy and Theoretical Computer Science*. CSAIL, MIT.

Laird, J. E., Gluck, K., Anderson, J., Forbus, K. D., Jenkins, O. C., Lebiere, C., ... Wray, R. E. (2017). Interactive task learning. *IEEE Intelligent Systems*, 32(4), 6–21.

Laird, J., Lebiere, C., & Rosenbloom, P. (2017). A standard model of the mind: Toward a common computational framework across artificial intelligence, cognitive science, neuroscience, and robotics. *AI Magazine*, 38(4). doi:10.1609/aimag.v38i4.2744.

Laird, J. (2012). *The SOAR Cognitive Architecture*. Cambridge, MA: The MIT Press.

Laird, J. E., Newell, A., & Rosenbloom, P. S. (1987). Soar: An architecture for general intelligence. *Artificial Intelligence*, 33, 1–64.

Lake, B. M., Ullman, T. D., Tenenbaum, J. B., & Gershman, S. J. (2017). Building machines that learn and think like people. *Behavioral and Brain Sciences*, 40, 1–72.

Langley, P. (2019). Scientific discovery, causal explanation, and process model induction. *Mind & Society*, 18, 43–56.

Langley, P. (2017). Interactive cognitive systems and social intelligence. *IEEE Intelligent Systems*, 32(4), 22–30.

Langley, P. (2012). The cognitive systems paradigm. *Advances in Cognitive Systems*, 1, 3–13.

Langley, P., Laird, J. E., & Rogers, S. (2009). Cognitive architectures: Research issues and challenges. *Cognitive Systems Research*, 10(2), 141–160.

Langley, P., Bradshaw, G. L., & Simon, H. A. (1983). Rediscovering chemistry with the BACON system. In *Machine Learning* (pp. 307–329). Berlin and Heidelberg: Springer.

Lenat, D. B. (1995). Cyc: A large-scale investment in knowledge infrastructure. *Communications of the ACM*, 38(11), 33–38.

Levesque, H. J. (2017). *Common Sense, the Turing Test, and the Quest for Real AI*. MIT Press.

Levesque, H., Davis, E., & Morgenstern, L. (2012). The winograd schema challenge. In *Thirteenth International Conference on the Principles of Knowledge Representation and Reasoning* (pp. 552–561). AAAI press.

Lieder, F., & Griffiths, T. L. (2019). Resource-rational analysis: Understanding human cognition as the optimal use of limited computational resources. *Behavioral and Brain Sciences* (43), 1–85.

Lieto, A., & Pozzato, G. L. (2020). A description logic framework for commonsense conceptual combination integrating typicality, probabilities and cognitive heuristics. *Journal of Experimental & Theoretical Artificial Intelligence*, 32(5), 769–804.

Lieto, A. (2020). Bounded rationality and heuristics in humans and in artificial cognitive systems. *Isonomia*, 2037, 4348.

Lieto, A., Perrone, F., Pozzato, G. L., & Chiodino, E. (2019). Beyond subgoaling: A dynamic knowledge generation framework for creative problem solving in cognitive architectures. *Cognitive Systems Research*, 58, 305–316.

Lieto, A. (2019). Heterogeneous proxytypes extended: Integrating theory-like representations and mechanisms with prototypes and exemplars. In *Biologically Inspired Cognitive Architectures Meeting* (pp. 217–227). Cham: Springer.

Lieto, A., Lebiere, C., & Oltramari, A. (2018). The knowledge level in cognitive architectures: Current limitations and possible developments. *Cognitive Systems Research*, 48, 39–55.

Lieto, A., Bhatt, M., Oltramari, A., & Vernon, D. (2018). The role of cognitive architectures in general artificial intelligence. *Cognitive Systems Research*, 48, 1–3.

Lieto, A., Radicioni, D. P., & Rho, V. (2017). Dual PECCS: A cognitive system for conceptual representation and categorization. *Journal of Experimental & Theoretical Artificial Intelligence*, 29(2), 433–452.

Lieto, A. (2017). Representational limits in cognitive architectures. In *EUCognition Meeting (European Society for Cognitive Systems) "Cognitive Robot Architectures"* (Vol. 1855, pp. 16–20). Ceur-ws.

Lieto, A., Radicioni, D., Rho, V., & Mensa, E. (2017). Towards a unifying framework for conceptual representation and reasoning in cognitive systems. *Intelligenza Artificiale*, 11(2), 139–153.

Lieto, A., Radicioni, D. P., & Rho, V. (2015). A common-sense conceptual categorization system integrating heterogeneous proxytypes and the dual process of reasoning. In *24th International Joint Conference on Artificial Intelligence (IJCAI 2015)* (pp. 875–881). AAAI Press.

Lieto, A. (2014). A computational framework for concept representation in cognitive systems and architectures: Concepts as heterogeneous proxytypes, *Procedia Computer Science*, 41, 6–14.

Malt, B. (1989). An on-line investigation of prototype and exemplar strategies in classification. *Journal of Experimental Psychology: Learning, Memory, and Cognition*, 15(4), 539.

Marr, D. (1982). *Vision*. San Francisco, CA: W. H. Freeman.

McCarthy, J. (2007). From here to human-level AI. *Artificial Intelligence*, 171, 1174–1182.

McCarthy, J. (1980). Circumscription: A form of non-monotonic reasoning. *Artificial intelligence*, 13(1–2), 27–39.

McCarthy, J., & Hayes, P. (1969). Some philosophical problems from the standpoint of artificial intelligence. In B. Meltzer & D. Michie (eds.), *Machine Intelligence* (Vol. 4). Edinburgh: Edinburgh University Press.

McCarthy, J. (1960). *Programs with Common Sense* (pp. 300–307). RLE and MIT Computation Center.

McCarthy, J., Minsky, M. L., Rochester, N., & Shannon, C. E. (1955). A proposal for the Dartmouth summer research project on artificial intelligence. *AI Magazine*, 27(4), 12–14.

McClelland, J. L. (2010). Emergence in cognitive science. *Topics in Cognitive Science*, 2(4), 751–770.

McCulloch, W. S., & Pitts, W. (1943). A logical calculus of the ideas immanent in nervous activity. *Bulletin of Mathematical Biophysics*, 5, 115–137. Reprinted in J. A. Anderson and E. Rosenfeld (1988).

McNamara, T. P. (2005). *Semantic Priming: Perspectives from Memory and Word Recognition*. Psychology Press.

Metta, G., Natale, L., Nori, F., Sandini, G., Vernon, D., Fadiga, L., & Bernardino, A. (2010). The iCub humanoid robot: An open-systems platform for research in cognitive development. *Neural Networks*, 23(8–9), 1125–1134.

Mikolov, T., Sutskever, I., Chen, K., Corrado, G. S., & Dean, J. (2013). Distributed representations of words and phrases and their compositionality. In *Advances in Neural Information Processing Systems* (pp. 3111–3119).

Miller, T. (2019). Explanation in artificial intelligence: Insights from the social sciences. *Artificial Intelligence*, 267, 1–38.

Miller, G. A. (1956). The magical number seven. *Psychological Review*, 63, 81.

Miller, G. A. (1995). WordNet: A lexical database for English. *Communications of the ACM*, 38(11), 39–41.

Minkowski, M. (2013). *Explaining the Computational Mind*. MIT Press.

Minsky, M. (2007). *The Emotion Machine: Commonsense Thinking, Artificial Intelligence, and the Future of the Human Mind*. Simon and Schuster.

Minsky, M. (1986). *The Society of Mind*. New York: Simon & Schuster.

Minsky, M. (1975). A framework for representing knowledge. In *The Psychology of Computer Vision*. New York: McGraw-Hill.

Minsky, M. L., & Papert, S. (1969). *Perceptrons*. Cambridge, MA: MIT Press.

Morgenstern, O., & Von Neumann, J. (1953). *Theory of Games and Economic Behavior.* Princeton University Press.

Murphy, G. (2002). *The Big Book of Concepts.* MIT Press.

Newell, A. (1990). *Unified Theories of Cognition.* Cambridge, MA: Harvard University Press.

Newell, A. (1988). The intentional stance and the knowledge level. *Behavioral and Brain Sciences,* 11(3), 520–522.

Newell, A. (1982). The knowledge level. *Artificial Intelligence,* 75, 87–127.

Newell, A. (1980). Physical symbol systems. *Cognitive Science,* 4, 135–83.

Newell A., & Simon, H. A. (1976). Computer science as empirical inquiry: Symbols and search. *Communications of the ACM,* 19(3), 113–126.

Newell, A. (1973). You can't play a game of 20 questions with nature and win. *Visual Information Processing,* 238–308.

Newell, A., & Simon, H. A. (1972). *Human Problem Solving.* Englewood Cliffs, NJ: Prentice-Hall.

Newell, A., Shaw, J. C., & Simon, H. A. (1959). Elements of a theory of human problem-solving, *Psychological Review,* 65, 151–166.

Nilsson, N. J. (1971). *Problem Solving Methods in Artificial Intelligence.* New York: McGraw-Hill.

Ohlsson, S., Sloan, Turán, G., Uber, D., & Urasky, A. (2012). An approach to evaluate AI commonsense reasoning systems. In *FLAIRS Conference* (pp. 371–374). AAAI press.

Pearl, J., & Mackenzie, D. (2018). *The Book of Why: The New Science of Cause and Effect.* Basic Books.

Pearl, J. (2009). *Causality.* Cambridge University Press.

Pennington, J., Socher, R., & Manning, C. D. (2014). Glove: Global vectors for word representation. In *Proceedings of the 2014 Conference on Empirical Methods in Natural Language Processing (EMNLP)* (pp. 1532–1543).

Picard, R. W. (1997). *Affective Computing.* MIT Press.

Piccinini, G. (2007). Computational modelling vs. Computational explanation: Is everything a Turing Machine, and does it matter to the philosophy of mind? *Australasian Journal of Philosophy,* 85(1), 93–115.

Pinker, S., & Prince, A. (1988). On language and connectionism: Analysis of a parallel distributed processing model of language acquisition. *Cognition,* 28(1–2), 73–193.

Putnam, H. (1960). *Minds and Machines.*

Pylyshyn, Z. W. (1989). Computing in cognitive science. In M. I. Posner (ed.), *Foundations of Cognitive Science* (pp. 51–91). Cambridge, MA: The MIT Press.

Pylyshyn, Z. W. (1984). *Computation and Cognition: Toward a Foundation for Cognitive Science.* Cambridge, MA: MIT Press.

Pylyshyn, Z. W. (1979). Complexity and the study of artificial and human intelligence. In M. Ringle (ed.), *Philosophical Perspectives in Artificial Intelligence.* Brighton: Harvester.

Quillian, M. R. (1968). Semantic memory. In M. Minsky (ed.), *Semantic Information Processing.* Cambridge, MA: MIT Press.

Reiter, R. (1980). A logic for default reasoning. *Artificial Intelligence,* 13(1–2), 81–132.

Rich, P., Blokpoel, M., de Haan, R., & van Rooij, I. (2020). How intractability spans the cognitive and evolutionary levels of explanation. *Topics in Cognitive Science* (12), 1382–1402.

Rosch, E. (1975). Cognitive representations of semantic categories. *Journal of Exerimental Psychology General,* 104(3), 192–233.

Rosenblatt, F. (1958). The Perceptron: A probabilistic model for information storage and organization in the brain, *Psychological Review*, 65, 386–408.

Rosenbloom, P. S. (2013). The Sigma cognitive architecture and system. *AISB Quarterly*, 136, 4–13.

Rosenblueth, A., & Wiener, N. (1945). The role of models in science. *Philosophy of Science*, 12, 316–321.

Rosenblueth, A., Wiener, N., & Bigelow, J. (1943). Behavior, purpose and teleology. *Philosophy of Science*, 10, 18–24.

Rumelhart, D. E., McClelland, J. L., & the PDP Research Group. (1986). *Parallel Distributed Processing: Explorations in the Microstructure of Cognition* (2 vols.). Cambridge, MA: MIT Press.

Russell S. J., & Norvig, P. (2002). *Artificial Intelligence: A Modern Approach* (2nd ed.).: Prentice Hall.

Russell, S. J., & Subramanian, D. (1995). Provably bounded-optimal agents. *Journal of Artificial Intelligence Research*, 2, 575–609.

Salvucci, D. (2014). Endowing a cognitive architecture with world knowledge. *Proceedings of the Annual Meeting of the Cognitive Science Society*, 36(36), 1353–1358.

Samuel, A. L. (1959). Machine learning. *The Technology Review*, 62(1), 42–45.

Schank, R. C., & Abelson, R. P. (1977). *Scripts, Plans, Goals and Understanding*. Hillsdale, NJ: Erlbaum.

Schank, R. C., & Nash-Webber, B. L. (eds.). (1975). *Theoretical Issues in Natural Language Processing*. Cambridge, MA: Bolt, Beranek and Newman.

Schank, R. C. (1972). Conceptual dependency: A theory of natural language understanding. *Cognitive Psychology*, 3, 552–631.

Searle, J. (1999). 'The Chinese Room'. In R. A. Wilson & F. Keil (eds.), *The MIT Encyclopedia of the Cognitive Sciences*. Cambridge, MA: MIT Press.

Searle, J. (1980). Minds, brains and programs. *Behavioral and Brain Sciences*, 3, 417–57.

Shayani, H. (2013). *A Practical Investigation into Achieving Bio-Plausibility in Evo-Devo Neural Microcircuits Feasible in an FPGA*. PhD Thesis. UCL.

Silver, D., Schrittwieser, J., Simonyan, K., Antonoglou, I., Huang, A., Guez, A., ... Chen, Y. (2017). Mastering the game of go without human knowledge. *Nature*, 550(7676), 354–359.

Simon, H. A. (1981). *The Sciences of the Artificial* (2nd ed.). Cambridge, MA: MIT Press.

Simon, H. A. (1979). *Models of Thought* (Vol. 352). Yale University Press.

Simon, H. A. (1955). A behavioral model of rational choice. *The Quarterly Journal of Economics*, 69(1), 99–118.

Simon, H. A. (1947). *Administrative Behavior: A Study of Decision-Making Processes in Administrative Organization*. New York: Macmillan.

Sloman, A. (2014). How can we reduce the gulf between artificial and natural intelligence? In *AIC, 2nd International Workshop on Artificial Intelligence and Cognition, Turin* (pp. 1–13).

Sloman, A. (2002). How many separately evolved emotional beasties live within us? In R. Trappl, P. Petta, & S. Payr (eds.), *Emotions in Humans and Artifacts* (pp. 29–96). Cambridge, MA: MIT Press.

Sloman, A. (2001). Beyond shallow models of emotion. *Cognitive Processing: International Quarterly of Cognitive Science*, 2(1), 177–198.

Sloman, A. (1998). Damasio, Descartes, alarms and meta-management. In *SMC'98 Conference Proceedings. 1998 IEEE International Conference on Systems, Man, and Cybernetics (Cat. No. 98CH36218)* (Vol. 3, pp. 2652–2657). IEEE.

Smith, J. D., & Minda, J. P. (1998). Prototypes in the mist: The early epochs of category learning. *Journal of Experimental Psychology: Learning, Memory, and Cognition*, 24(6), 1411.

Smith, J. D., Murray, M. J., & Minda, J. P. (1997). Straight talk about linear separability. *Journal of Experimental Psychology: Learning, Memory, and Cognition*, 23, 659–668.

Su, Jiawei, Danilo Vasconcellos Vargas, and Kouichi Sakurai. "One pixel attack for fooling deep neural networks." IEEE Transactions on Evolutionary Computation 23.5 (2017): 828–841.

Sun, R. (2007). The importance of cognitive architectures: An analysis based on CLARION. *Journal of Experimental & Theoretical Artificial Intelligence*, 19(2), 159–193.

Sun, R. (2004). Desiderata for cognitive architectures. *Philosophical Psychology*, 17(3), 341–373.

Susanto, Y., Livingstone, A., Ng, B. C., & Cambria, E. (2020). The Hourglass model revisited. *IEEE Intelligent Systems*, 35(5), 96–102.

Turing A. M. (1950). Computing machinery and intelligence. *Mind*, 59(236), 433–460.

Turing, A. M. (1936–37). On computable numbers, with an application to the Entscheidungs problem. *Proceeding of the London Mathematical Society*, 42, 230–265; 43, 544.

Tversky, A., & Kahneman, D. (1983). Extension versus intuitive reasoning: The conjunction fallacy in probability judgment. *Psychological Review*, 90(4), 293–315.

Van Fraassen, B. C. (1980). *The Scientific Image*. Oxford: Clarendon Press.

Veale, T., & Cardoso, F. A. (eds.). (2019). *Computational Creativity: The Philosophy and Engineering of Autonomously Creative Systems*. Springer.

Vernon, D., von Hofsten, C., & Fadiga, L. (2017). Desiderata for developmental cognitive architectures. *Biologically Inspired Cognitive Architectures*, 18, 116–127.

Vernon, D. (2014). *Artificial Cognitive Systems: A Primer*. MIT Press.

Wallin, A., & Gärdenfors, P. (2000). Smart people who make simple heuristics work. *Behavioral and Brain Sciences*, 23(5), 765–765.

Watson, J. B. (1913). Psychology as the behaviorist views it. *Psychological Review*, 20, 158–177.

Webb, B. (2001). Can robots make good models of biological behaviour? *Behavioral and Brain Sciences*, 24(6), 1033–1050.

Weizenbaum, J. (1966). ELIZA—a computer program for the study of natural language communication between man and machine. *Communications of the ACM*, 9(1), 36–45.

Weizenbaum, J. (1976). *Computer Power and Human Reason*. San Francisco, CA: Freeman.

Wiener, N. (1948/1961). *Cybernetics, or Control and Communication in the Animal and the Machine* (2nd ed.). Cambridge, MA: MIT Press.

Winograd, T. (1972). *Understanding Natural Language*. Academic Press: New York.

Winston, P. H. (2014). *The Genesis Story Understanding and Story Telling System a 21st Century Step Toward Artificial Intelligence*. Center for Brains, Minds and Machines (CBMM).

Winston, P. H. (2012a). The next 50 years: A personal view. *Biologically Inspired Cognitive Architectures*, 1, 92–99.

Winston, P. H. (2012b). The right way. *Advances in Cognitive Systems*, 1, 23–36.

Winston, P. H. (2011). The strong story hypothesis and the directed perception hypothesis. In P. Langley (ed.), *Papers from the AAAI Fall Symposium* (pp. 345–352), Technical Report FS-11-01. Menlo Park, CA: AAAI Press.

Zaadnoordijk, L., Besold, T. R., & Cusack, R. (2020). The next big thing(s) in unsupervised machine learning: Five lessons from infant learning. *arXiv preprint arXiv:2009.08497*.

Zadeh, L. A. (1988). Fuzzy logic. *Computer*, 21(4), 83–93.

INDEX

A* algorithm 13
ACT-R 40, 61, 63–65, 69, 70–72, 75, 86, 103
Adaptive Toolbox (AT) Theory 42–43
Advice Taker 39
AIC (Artificial Intelligence and Cognition Workshop Series) 105
Artificial Intelligence (AI) 1–2, 10, 19–20, 43, 52, 54, 57–58, 89
Alpha Go 52–57, 60
Alpha Go Zero 53
Alpha Zero 54, 56
Anderson, J. A. 40, 42, 63–65, 71, 85–86
Allen (the robot) 16
Ant metaphor 15–56
Artificial neural networks (ANNs) 4, 17, 24, 32–33, 49
Automata w. negative-feedback 47; *see also* servomechanisms

Backpropagation 15, 32
Bartlett, F. C. 5; *see also* Memory schema
Behaviorism 11
Bigelow, J. 47
Bhatt, M. 57–58
Biological plausibility 31, 33, 47, 48
Boden, M. A. 101
Bounded rationality 3, 5, 38–39
Braitenberg, V. 46–47
Breazeal, C. 102
Brooks, R. 8, 16–17, 89

Caenorhabditis elegans 23
Carnegie Mellon University 3, 7

Catastrophic interference 96
Checkers 10
Chinese Room 83–84
Chomsky, N. 15
Churchland, P. M. 32
Churchland, P. S. 32, 84
Clarion 59
Cognitive architecture 7, 15, 40, 57–66, 69–72, 74–75, 85, 93, 100
Cognitive computing 19, 22–23, 52–54
Cognitive modelling 9, 13, 15, 18, 23, 36–38, 43–46, 49, 51, 58, 61, 84, 94, 103
Cognitive plausibility 20, 50, 89
Cognitive psychology 1, 3, 10, 18, 61
Cognitive robotics 93, 104
Cognitive science 1–2, 4–5, 9, 12, 18, 25, 27, 31, 43, 48, 54, 57, 66, 71, 87, 93–95
Common Model of Cognition 103, 105; *see also* Standard Model of Mind
Commonsense reasoning 5–6, 13, 17, 23, 34–35, 70, 74–76, 95, 97–99
Companions 101
Compositionality 11–13, 17
Computationalism 29
Computational creativity 13, 19, 95, 101
Computational models of cognition 9, 19, 32, 44, 76, 84, 87
Conceptual dependency theory 6
Conceptual spaces 72–73, 75
Conjunction fallacy 39, 81
Convolutional neural networks 56
CopyCat 99
Cordeschi, R. 4, 9–10, 14–15, 23, 25, 29, 31, 35, 47, 80

Crick, F. 32
Creature hypothesis 16
Cryptoarithmetic problems 36
Cybernetics 9, 33, 47
CYC 71, 73–74

DARPA 77, 89, 97; challenge 77, 89
Dartmouth workshop 2
Davis, E. 74, 87, 98
Deep Blue 53, 54
Deep learning 17, 32, 33, 43, 53, 56, 84, 96,
    98–99
Deep neural networks 32, 53, 96, 100
Design stance 28
Dennett, D. C. 28–30, 46
Diagrammatic representations 4
Distributional Semantics 72
Dreyfus, H. 18
Dynamic systems 14
DUAL PECCS 72–76, 98
Dual process theory 72, 74

Eliasmith, C. 71
ELIZA 8, 79
Emotion modelling 95, 102
Emergentist approaches 8, 13
Enactive approaches 13
Exemplars theory 66–67
Explanation 2, 23, 26, 29, 43, 50; models of
    43–49

Field Programmable Gate Arrays
    (FPGAs) 34
Fodor, J. 29
Folk psychology 46, 79
Forbus, K. 101
Frames 4–5
Frixione, M. 29, 38, 80–82
Frame problem 17
Functional equivalence 22, 31
Functionalism 21, 23–24, 30
Functional/structural ratio 50, 54, 75
Fuzzy logic 35

Gardner, H. 80
Gärdenfors, P. 43, 72
Gigerenzer, G. 38, 42
Genesis (system) 97
Genetic algorithms 33
GOFAI, (Good-Old-Fashioned-AI) 8
GPS (General Problem Solver) 2–3, 7–8,
    10, 13, 35, 61
GPT-3 99
GPUs (Graphical Processing Units) 34

Hayes, P. J. 17
Harnad, S. 17, 80
Hebb, D. O. 14
Herbert (robot) 8
Heuristic(s) 2–3, 7–10, 13, 18, 20, 33–36,
    39, 42–43, 54, 61–62, 76, 81, 86, 89, 98;
    means-end 2
Hinton, G. 15
Hofstadter, D. R. 99
Holland, J. H. 33
Hopfield, J. J. 14
Human Brain Project 23
Hybrid systems 17

IBM Watson 22, 44, 52
iCub 102
Information Processing Psychology (IPP)
    9, 11, 15
IIT (Istituto Italiano di Tecnologia) 60
Interactive Task Learning 96
Intentional stance 26, 28–30, 84

Johnson-Laird, P. N. 4, 81

Kahneman, D. 38–39, 74, 98
Kasparov, G. 53–54
Kismet 102
Knowledge level 27, 29–30, 65, 70, 85

Laird, J. 7, 59, 61, 70, 96, 103
Langley, P. 7–8, 59–60, 101
Lebiere, C. 65, 71, 85, 103
Levesque, H. 79, 87
Lieto, A. 5, 7, 13, 58, 65, 69–72, 76

Machine learning 19, 32, 95–96, 101–102
Marcus, G. 74, 98–99
MARGIE 6
Marr, D. 24–28, 31, 38, 41, 42, 89
McCarthy, J. 2–3, 5, 17, 19, 35
McClelland, J. 13, 15, 32
Memory schema 5
Metta, G. 60
MIT, Massachussets Institute of Technology
    8, 10, 16, 56, 62, 97
Mimimal Cognitive Grid (MCG) 37, 48,
    50–54, 54–56, 65, 75, 90, 94
Minimax algorithm 67–68
Minsky, M. L. 2–7, 10, 14–15, 18, 34
Mitchell, M. 99
Monte Carlo Tree Search 53
Morgenstern, L. 87
Morgenstern, O. 38
Multi-agent systems 89

Multiple realizability 22; *see also* Functionalism
Multiple intelligence theory 80

Newell, A. 2–3, 7, 9–11, 15, 22, 27–30, 36, 57, 61–63, 65, 77, 81, 85
Newell test 77, 85–86, 90
Neuromorphing computing 49

Oltramari, A. 57–58, 65, 71
Operant conditioning 11, 54; *see also* Reinforcement learning

Papert, S. 14–15
PDP (Parallel Distributed Processing) 14–15, 32
Perceptron 14
Physical Symbol System Hypothesis 10–13, 26, 83
Prototype theory 5, 66
Pylyshyn Z. 12, 17, 23, 25–29

Quillian, M. R. 3–4

Rational Analysis (RA) 39, 42, 65
Reinforcement learning 53, 60
Robocup 77, 89
Robocup@home 90
Rochester, N. 2
Rosch, E. 5, 12, 66
Rosenblatt, F. 14–15
Rosenbloom, P. 7, 103
Rosenblueth, A. 23, 47
Rumelhart, D. 14–15, 32

SAM (Script Applier Mechanism) 6
Samuel, A. 10
Sandini, G. 60
Schank, R. C. 6, 18
Scientific Sense podcast 75
Scripts 6, 97

Searle, J. R. 83–85
Self-organizing systems 10
Semantic networks 3, 13, 44, 70, 73
Semantic priming 81
Shakey (robot) 13, 89
Shannon, C. 2
Shayani, H. 33–34
SHRDLU 6–7
Simon, H. A. 2–3, 9–11, 15, 21, 29, 36, 38, 43, 56–57
Society of mind 7
Spatial cognition 4
Spreading activation 3–4
Standard Model of Mind 103–105
Strong Story Hypothesis 97
Strong vs Weak AI 84
Structure mapping engine 101
Subsumption architecture 8, 16–17
Sun, R. 58–59
Supervised learning 60
Symbol grounding problem 17

Thinking-aloud protocol 2, 36
Total Turing Test 80, 90–91
Transfer learning 54, 95, 101
Turing, A. M. 14
Turing Test 77, 78, 83, 90

Unsupervised learning 60, 95

Vernon, D. 8, 10, 12–13, 30, 57–58, 60
Von Neumann, J. 11, 38

Webb, B. 48–51
Wiener, N. 9, 23, 47
Winograd, T. 6
Winograd Schema Challenge 77, 87, 90, 92
Winston, P. 97
Wordnet 70, 72, 75

Zadeh, L. 35

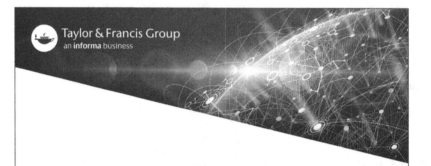

Printed in the United States
By Bookmasters